# TEACHER'S PET PUBLICATIONS

# LITPLAN TEACHER PACK
for
The Crucible
based on the play by
Arthur Miller

Written by
Mary B. Collins

© 1997 Teacher's Pet Publications
All Rights Reserved

ISBN 978-1-60249-147-2

This **LitPlan** for Arthur Miller's
*The Crucible*
has been brought to you by Teacher's Pet Publications

Copyright Teacher's Pet Publications 1997


Only the student materials in this unit plan
such as worksheets, study questions, assignment sheets, and tests
may be reproduced multiple times for use in the purchaser's classroom.

For any additional copyright questions,
contact Teacher's Pet Publications.


www.tpet.com

# TABLE OF CONTENTS - *The Crucible*

| | |
|---|---|
| Introduction | 5 |
| Unit Objectives | 8 |
| Reading Assignment Sheet | 9 |
| Unit Outline | 10 |
| Study Questions (Short Answer) | 13 |
| Quiz/Study Questions (Multiple Choice) | 24 |
| Pre-reading Vocabulary Worksheets | 37 |
| Lesson One (Introductory Lesson) | 53 |
| Nonfiction Assignment Sheet | 55 |
| Oral Reading Evaluation Form | 57 |
| Writing Assignment 1 | 67 |
| Writing Assignment 2 | 70 |
| Writing Assignment 3 | 81 |
| Writing Evaluation Form | 71 |
| Vocabulary Review Activities | 64 |
| Extra Writing Assignments/Discussion ?s | 73 |
| Unit Review Activities | 78 |
| Unit Tests | 82 |
| Unit Resource Materials | 113 |
| Vocabulary Resource Materials | 127 |

# A FEW NOTES ABOUT THE AUTHOR
# ARTHUR MILLER

Mr. Miller was born in Harlem (New York) on October 17, 1915. He attended public schools, but quit before graduation. He held odd jobs such as farmhand, laborer, etc. Later, he got into The University of Michigan where he wrote and attended classes. In 1938 he graduated from The University of Michigan.

In 1949 Mr. Miller won the Pulitzer Prize for *Death of a Salesman*. In 1953 *The Crucible* was produced on Broadway. Other notable works by Arthur Miller include *All My Sons, After The Fall, A View From The Bridge, The Price, Incident at Vichy,* and *The Misfits* (a movie starring Marilyn Monroe, to whom he was once married.)

--- Courtesy of Compton's Learning Company

# INTRODUCTION - *The Crucible*

This unit has been designed to develop students' reading, writing, thinking, and language skills through exercises and activities related to *The Crucible* by Arthur Miller. It includes nineteen lessons, supported by extra resource materials.

The **introductory lesson** introduces students to the Puritans and witchcraft via a student-reporting and bulletin board-making activity. Following the introductory activity, students are given a transition to explain how the activity relates to the book they are about to read. Following the transition, students are given the materials they will be using during the unit. At the end of the lesson, students begin the pre-reading work for the first reading assignment.

The **reading assignments** are done orally for this play. The parts to be spoken during each class session are listed on each lesson page. The teacher only needs to assign students to each part. Students have approximately 15 minutes of pre-reading work to do prior to each reading assignment. This pre-reading work involves reviewing the study questions for the assignment and doing some vocabulary work for 8 to 10 vocabulary words they will encounter in their reading.

The **study guide questions** are fact-based questions; students can find the answers to these questions right in the text. These questions come in two formats: short answer or multiple choice. The best use of these materials is probably to use the short answer version of the questions as study guides for students (since answers will be more complete), and to use the multiple choice version for occasional quizzes. If your school has the appropriate equipment, it might be a good idea to make transparencies of your answer keys for the overhead projector.

The **vocabulary work** is intended to enrich students' vocabularies as well as to aid in the students' understanding of the book. Prior to each reading assignment, students will complete a two-part worksheet for approximately 8 to 10 vocabulary words in the upcoming reading assignment. Part I focuses on students' use of general knowledge and contextual clues by giving the sentence in which the word appears in the text. Students are then to write down what they think the words mean based on the words' usage. Part II nails down the definitions of the words by giving students dictionary definitions of the words and having students match the words to the correct definitions based on the words' contextual usage. Students should then have a thorough understanding of the words when they meet them in the text.

After each reading assignment, students will go back and formulate answers for the study guide questions. Discussion of these questions serves as a **review** of the most important events and ideas presented in the reading assignments.

After students complete reading the work, there is a **vocabulary review** lesson which pulls together all of the fragmented vocabulary lists for the reading assignments and gives students a review of all of the words they have studied.

The **group activity** which follows the vocabulary review has students working in small groups to discuss several important aspects of the play. Using the information they have acquired so far through individual work and class discussions, students get together to further examine the text and to brainstorm ideas relating to five specific aspects of the play.

The group activity is followed by a **reports and discussion** session in which the groups share their ideas about their topics with the entire class; thus, the entire class is exposed to information about all of the topics and the entire class can discuss each topic based on the nucleus of information brought forth by each of the groups.

Two lessons are devoted to **creating and performing a scene** in which Abigail is on trial for being the cause of death for those who died during the witch trials.

A lesson is devoted to the **extra discussion questions/writing assignments**. These questions focus on interpretation, critical analysis and personal response, employing a variety of thinking skills and adding to the students' understanding of the play.

There are three **writing assignments** in this unit, each with the purpose of informing, persuading, or having students express personal opinions. The first assignment is to inform: students write a composition based upon their theme topics. The second assignment is to persuade: students are given a choice of letters to write from one character to another, persuading him or her of something. (The topic is given in the letter assignment.) The third assignment is to give students a chance to simply express their own opinions: following the unit test, students write a composition explaining who, in their opinion, is responsible for the Salem witch trials.

In addition, there is a **nonfiction reading assignment**. Students are required to read a piece of nonfiction related in some way to *The Crucible* (articles about witchcraft, Puritanism, theocracies, our judicial system, trial transcripts, etc.). After reading their nonfiction pieces, students will fill out a worksheet on which they answer questions regarding facts, interpretation, criticism, and personal opinions. During one class period, students make **oral presentations** about the nonfiction pieces they have read. This not only exposes all students to a wealth of information, it also gives students the opportunity to practice **public speaking**.

The **review lesson** pulls together all of the aspects of the unit. The teacher is given four or five choices of activities or games to use which all serve the same basic function of reviewing all of the information presented in the unit.

The **unit test** comes in two formats: all multiple choice-matching-true/false or with a mixture of matching, short answer, multiple choice, and composition. As a convenience, two different tests for each format have been included.

There are additional **support materials** included with this unit. The **extra activities packet** includes suggestions for an in-class library, crossword and word search puzzles related to the play, and extra vocabulary worksheets. There is a list of **bulletin board ideas** which gives the teacher suggestions for bulletin boards to go along with this unit. In addition, there is a list of **extra class activities** the teacher could choose from to enhance the unit or as a substitution for an exercise the teacher might feel is inappropriate for his/her class. **Answer keys** are located directly after the **reproducible student materials** throughout the unit. The student materials may be reproduced for use in the teacher's classroom without infringement of copyrights. No other portion of this unit may be reproduced without the written consent of Teacher's Pet Publications.

# UNIT OBJECTIVES - *The Crucible*

1. Through reading Miller's *The Crucible*, students will gain a better understanding of the Salem witch trials and the Puritans.

2. Students will demonstrate their understanding of the text on four levels: factual, interpretive, critical and personal.

3. Students will consider the themes of crime and punishment, individual vs. authority, and revenge.

4. Students will be exposed to a different era of American life, showing many of today's conflicts are not new; they are rooted in our American past.

5. As they are exposed to the path of John Proctor's personal development, students will learn about a citizen's responsibility to become involved in his world.

6. Students will be given the opportunity to practice reading aloud to improve their oral reading skills.

7. Students will answer questions to demonstrate their knowledge and understanding of the main events and characters in *The Crucible* as they relate to the author's theme development.

8. Students will enrich their vocabularies and improve their understanding of the play through the vocabulary lessons prepared for use in conjunction with the play.

9. The writing assignments in this unit are geared to several purposes:
    a. To have students demonstrate their abilities to inform, to persuade, or to express their own personal ideas

        Note: Students will demonstrate ability to write effectively to <u>inform</u> by developing and organizing facts to convey information. Students will demonstrate the ability to write effectively to <u>persuade</u> by selecting and organizing relevant information, establishing an argumentative purpose, and by designing an appropriate strategy for an identified audience. Students will demonstrate the ability to write effectively to <u>express personal ideas</u> by selecting a form and its appropriate elements.

    b. To check the students' reading comprehension
    c. To make students think about the ideas presented by the play
    d. To encourage logical thinking
    e. To provide an opportunity to practice good grammar and improve students' use of the English language.

# READING ASSIGNMENT SHEET - *The Crucible*

| Date Assigned | Reading Assignment | Completion Date |
|---|---|---|
| | Act One to Hale's Entrance | |
| | Hale's Entrance to End of Act One | |
| | Act Two to Giles's Entrance | |
| | Giles's Entrance to End of Act Two | |
| | Act Three to the Girls' Entrance | |
| | The Girls' Entrance to End of Act Three | |
| | Act Four | |

# UNIT OUTLINE - *The Crucible*

| 1<br><br>Introduction<br><br>PV Act I | 2<br><br>Read Act I Orally | 3<br><br>Finish Act I<br><br>Study ?s Act I | 4<br><br>PV Act II<br><br>Read Act II Orally | 5<br><br>Finish Act II<br><br>Study ?s Act II<br><br>PV Act III |
|---|---|---|---|---|
| 6<br><br>Read Act III Orally | 7<br><br>Finish Act III<br><br>Study ?s Act III<br><br>PV Act IV | 8<br><br>Read Act IV Orally | 9<br><br>Study ?s Act IV<br><br>Vocabulary Review | 10<br><br>Group Activity |
| 11<br><br>Reports & Discussion | 12<br><br>Writing Assignment 1 | 13<br><br>Project | 14<br><br>Project | 15<br><br>Writing Assignment 2<br><br>Writing Conf. |
| 16<br><br>Extra Discussion ?s | 17<br><br>Nonfiction Reports | 18<br><br>Writing Assignment 3 | 19<br><br>Review | 20<br><br>Test |

KEY:  P = preview study questions   V = vocabulary work   R = Read

# STUDY GUIDE QUESTIONS

This blank page is inserted for two-sided printing.

# SHORT ANSWER STUDY GUIDE QUESTIONS - *The Crucible*

Act One
1. "So now they and their church found it necessary to deny any other sect its freedom, lest their New Jerusalem be defiled and corrupted by wrong and deceitful ideas." What is the irony in that statement?
2. Explain how the witch-hunt years were a time of "general revenge."
3. Identify Tituba, Abigail, and Betty.
4. Why does Mrs. Putnam believe there are witches in Salem?
5. Why is Thomas Putnam bitter?
6. Parris says, "Oh, Abigail, what proper payment for my charity! Now I am undone!" What does that mean?
7. What is Mary's argument to Abby?
8. Describe Proctor.
9. What happened between Abigail and John Proctor prior to the opening of the play?
10. What was the "sign" that Betty was bewitched?
11. Identify Francis and Rebecca Nurse.
12. Explain the political relationship between the Putnam and Nurse families.
13. What did Rebecca do to Betty?
14. What is Rebecca's explanation of the girls' behavior?
15. "There are wheels within wheels in this village and fires within fires." Explain.
16. What is Proctor's reason for his not regularly attending church?
17. What does Parris want?
18. Giles says, "Think on it now, it's a deep thing, and dark as a pit." To what is he referring literally and symbolically?
19. What do Putnam and Proctor argue about? What does this show?
20. Who is Rev. John Hale, and why does he come to Salem?
21. Hale says, "They [the books] must be [heavy]; they are weighted with authority." What is the significance of this remark?
22. To what did Tituba confess? Why?
23. What do the girls do at the end of Act One?

*Crucible* Study Questions Page 2

Act Two
1. Where does Elizabeth want John to go, and what does she want him to do there?
2. What is John's response to her prodding?
3. What gift did Mary give Elizabeth?
4. What was the "evidence" against Sarah Good?
5. Why doesn't Proctor want Mary to go back to court?
6. Why does Elizabeth think Abigail wants to kill her?
7. Why did Hale come to Proctor's house?
8. What things are "suspicious" about Proctor and his family?
9. Hale asks Elizabeth if she believes in witches. What is her reply?
10. On what charge(s) was Rebecca Nurse arrested?
11. Why does Cheever come to the Proctor house?
12. Explain the significance of the needle in the "poppet."
13. What will happen to Proctor if he tries to discredit Abby?
14. Why doesn't Mary want to testify about the doll?


Act Three
1. Why do Giles and Francis want to talk to Danforth?
2. What is Parris's argument against Proctor?
3. What does Mary tell Danforth?
4. When Danforth hears that Elizabeth is pregnant, what does he allow?
5. What paper did ninety-one people sign?
6. ". . . a person is either with this court or he must be counted against it, there be no road between." Explain the importance of Danforth's statement.
7. What quote did Proctor use to help Mary remain brave?
8. Of what does Giles accuse Putnam?
9. What is Hale's problem as Proctor and his friends present evidence to Danforth?
10. Hawthorne thinks of a test for Mary. What is it? Can she do it? Why or why not?
11. Proctor calls Abigail a whore, and he confesses his lechery. Danforth tests Proctor's statement by calling for Elizabeth and asking her why Abigail was dismissed. What does Elizabeth say? Why?
12. What do the girls do to Mary? What is her response?
13. What happens to Proctor?
14. What does Hale do?

*Crucible* Study Questions Page 3

Act Four
1. What explanation does Cheever give for Parris' "mad look"?
2. What did Abigail do?
3. Parris says, "You cannot hang this sort. There is danger for me." What "sort" does he mean, and what is the danger to him?
4. Explain Danforth's reason that a pardon would not be just.
5. Why has Hale come back to Salem?
6. What does Hale want Elizabeth to do?
7. What happened to Giles?
8. Proctor says, "My honesty is broke, Elizabeth, I am no good man." Explain.
9. What "confession" did Elizabeth make to John?
10. What did Proctor do after he signed the confession? Why?
11. "I have given you my soul; leave me my name!" Explain.
12. "He have his goodness now. God forbid I take it from him!" What does Elizabeth mean?

# ANSWER KEY: SHORT ANSWER STUDY GUIDE QUESTIONS - *The Crucible*

<u>Act One</u>

1. "So now they and their church found it necessary to deny any other sect its freedom, lest their New Jerusalem be defiled and corrupted by wrong and deceitful ideas." What is the irony in that statement?

    The Puritans came to this country for religious freedom; however, when they got here they persecuted others as they had been persecuted. They turned their colony into a place almost as bad as the place they had left.

2. Explain how the witch-hunt years were a time of "general revenge." Being under such strict laws and commandments, the Puritans had to repress a lot of their anger and spirit of revenge towards their neighbors. When the witch hunts started, it was an excellent opportunity for them to "let their hair down" and get revenge on their neighbors for whatever petty squabbles they had been having.

3. Identify Tituba, Abigail, Betty

    Tituba was Parris' slave woman from Barbados. She went with the girls into the forest and was accused of conjuring spirits, accused of being a witch. Later, she confessed to being a witch to save her life.

    Abigail was Parris' niece. She lived with Parris because her own parents had been killed by Indians. Abigail was the main instigator of the witch hunt; she enjoyed the attention and tried to get revenge on several people in the village, particularly Elizabeth Proctor. She wanted to take Elizabeth's place as John Proctor's wife.

    Betty was Parris' daughter. In the opening scene, she has had some sort of a fit, and the only explanation the people of Salem can find for her condition is the presence of witchcraft in their village.

4. Why does Mrs. Putnam believe there are witches in Salem?

    She has lost many babies in their first few days of life, and the child of her only successful childbirth (Ruth) is acting peculiar. Witchcraft is her answer to these strange events.

5. Why is Thomas Putnam bitter?

    His candidate for minister was rejected, and his attempt to break his father's will had failed. He considered himself to be the intellectual superior to most of the people of Salem, and yet he often did not get his own way. He was a greedy, frustrated, bitter man.

6. Parris says, "Oh, Abigail, what proper payment for my charity! Now I am undone!" What does that mean?

   Parris was having troubles of his own before the story began. His controversial appointment had left his parish divided and argumentative. He was trying to keep everything together. Now, his niece's flirting with witchcraft would bring further doubts upon his ministry and give his enemies more ammunition against him. After he has taken her in and provided her with a home, she has done something which could likely cause his ruin.

7. What is Mary's argument to Abby?

   She wants Abby to tell the truth about the happenings in the woods. The worst that can happen to them would be that they would be spanked and reprimanded. She suspects that if the lies go on, things could get out of hand and the punishment would be far worse (jail or hanging).

8. Describe Proctor.

   Proctor is a strong, fit man in his thirties. He is a farmer. Basically he is an even-tempered man, soft-spoken, but full of authority and confidence.

9. What happened between Abigail and John Proctor prior to the opening of the play?

   They apparently had an affair.

10. What was the "sign" that Betty was bewitched? She could not stand to hear the Lord's name.

11. Identify Francis and Rebecca Nurse.

    Francis was a levelheaded man, greatly respected by many of the village people. He was known for his calm nature and abilities as an arbitrator. Rebecca, his wife, was a truly good woman, kind and gentle in her manner. Rebecca helped to deliver some of the Putnam's babies.

12. Explain the political relationship between the Putnam and Nurse families.

    The Nurses were not liked by the Putnams because of some land disputes, and this conflict was somewhat revenged by the Putnams when Ann Putnam accused Rebecca of bewitching her newborn babies (implying she was responsible for their deaths).

13. What did Rebecca do to Betty?

    She stood over Betty and quieted her.

14. What is Rebecca's explanation of the girls' behavior?

    She thinks the girls have made up their story to get some attention and that in a few days when the sport wears off, the whole thing should be forgotten. Not much attention should be paid to the girls.

15. "There are wheels within wheels in this village and fires within fires." Explain. There were many political and personal grudges held among the people of Salem, all mixed up with their social and religious beliefs. The whole affair was rather tangled and deep-rooted.

16. What is Proctor's reason for his not regularly attending church?
    He doesn't like Parris. He thinks there is too little mention of God in church and too much mention of fire and brimstone. He also doesn't think Parris is a very good minister because he seems too concerned with material wealth.

17. What does Parris want?
    Parris wanted the deed to his house, and firewood in addition to his salary.

18. Giles says, "Think on it now, it's a deep thing, and dark as a pit." To what is he referring literally and symbolically?
    Literally, he is talking about the fact that people are not getting along and are suing each other at an alarming rate. Symbolically, he is talking about the deeper-rooted problem that their system of theocracy seems to be failing.

19. What do Putnam and Proctor argue about? What does this show?
    They argue about lumber and the ownership of a piece of land on which the lumber grows. We are shown Putnam as a land-grabbing man who will use devious means to get what he wants.

20. Who is Rev. John Hale, and why does he come to Salem?
    Rev. John Hale is an expert in witchcraft. He comes to Salem to do what he can to help the town rid itself of witchcraft.

21. Hale says, "They [the books] must be [heavy]; they are weighted with authority." What is the significance of this remark?
    Symbolically, the books usually stand for education, learning, the educated. In this case, these books are filled with information about the devil and witchcraft (and how to get rid of it). It has not-very scientific and not-well-proven information, information which, we believe, is by its very nature, not substantial. Yet, the people of Salem and John Hale put their faith in it. In much the same way, they later place their faith in the girls and the girls become weighted with authority although they (the girls) have information that is not substantiated.

    Another possible symbolic interpretation would be an analogy between their faith in these books and their faith in the Bible. The books they believed in were, in effect, their law; they were from where the justification for the Puritan society originated. Because of this, they were weighted with authority.

22. To what did Tituba confess? Why?
   Tituba confessed that she conjured spirits and met with the devil and signed his book. Parris was leading her to give those answers. If she had not "confessed," she would have hanged.

23. What do the girls do at the end of Act One?
   They admit that they were bewitched, and they started naming the names of people they had seen with the devil.

Act Two
1. Where does Elizabeth want John to go, and what does she want him to do there?
   Elizabeth wants John to go into Salem to tell the authorities that the girls are not telling the truth.

2. What is John's response to her prodding?
   He is reluctant to go. He understands that he probably should go, but he does not want to get personally involved with the activity.

3. What gift did Mary give Elizabeth?
   Mary gave Elizabeth a "poppet" (doll) she had made while sitting in court.

4. What was the "evidence" against Sarah Good?
   She confessed to witchcraft. The girls said she nearly choked them to death (and they acted so) in court. She mumbled when after begging for cider and bread, she had been turned away. She could not recite the commandments in court.

5. Why doesn't Proctor want Mary to go back to court?
   If she goes back, that makes him further involved. Also, he believes that the accusations are false and the girls are frauds. It isn't a just court in Proctor's eyes.

6. Why does Elizabeth think Abigail wants to kill her?
   Elizabeth knows of John's affair with Abby. She believes that Abby wants to take her place as John's wife.

7. Why did Hale come to Proctor's house?
   Hale came out to question all accused persons for himself, so that he would have some knowledge of the people before they appeared in court or jail. He came to Proctor's house to question them to see if either of them had any suspicious activities which would relate to witchcraft.

8. What things are "suspicious" about Proctor and his family?
    Proctor does not go to church regularly. His youngest son has not been baptized. He does not have total faith in Parris, the minister. It takes both Parris and Elizabeth to remember all of the commandments. (He significantly forgot adultery.)

9. Hale asks Elizabeth if she believes in witches. What is her reply?
    If she is accused of being a witch, she cannot believe in witches. However, if the Bible says that witches exist, she cannot dispute the Bible.

10. On what charge(s) was Rebecca Nurse arrested?
    She was arrested for the "marvelous and supernatural murder of Goody Putnam's babies."

11. Why does Cheever come to the Proctor house?
    Cheever comes to arrest Elizabeth.

12. Explain the significance of the needle in the "poppet."
    Abigail had accused Elizabeth of sticking a needle in her (Abby's) stomach through the use of a "poppet" (doll). Cheever asked to see the doll that was in Elizabeth's house (the one that Mary had given her). When he looked under the dress, there was a needle stuck in the abdomen of the doll. On the basis of this evidence, Cheever determined that witchcraft was possible and did, in fact, take Elizabeth to prison.

13. What will happen to Proctor if he tries to discredit Abby?
    She will tell that they had an affair; she will discredit his name by calling him a lecher.

14. Why doesn't Mary want to testify about the doll?
    She doesn't want to testify because she is afraid of Abigail. She knows Abigail will "get her" if she goes against her.

Act Three
1. Why do Giles and Francis want to talk to Danforth?
    They go to try to persuade the judge that their wives are good women, not witches.

2. What is Parris' argument against Proctor?
    Parris says that Proctor is trying to overthrow the court.

3. What does Mary tell Danforth?
    "It were pretense, sir." The girls have been lying.

4. When Danforth hears that Elizabeth is pregnant, what does he allow?
    He allows her time to see if her "natural signs" appear. If they do not, and she is truly pregnant, he will allow her one year before she is hanged, to have her baby. The point is that if Proctor is just trying to save Elizabeth, he need not continue with his arguments; she is saved for another year.

5. What paper did ninety-one people sign?
    They signed that Rebecca, Elizabeth and Martha were all good, upstanding, God-loving citizens.

6. ". . . a person is either with this court or he must be counted against it, there be no road between." Explain the importance of Danforth's statement.
    Danforth (and the Puritan doctrine) left no room for in-between cases. Either people were witches or they weren't. There was no room for "appearances." If one opposed the court, one would be in contempt. There was no room for error on the part of the court and no room for question or correction of the court. It could, then, go on forever in its incorrect path.

7. What quote did Proctor use to help Mary remain brave?
    "Do that which is good, and no harm will come to thee." It is ironic in a layman's point of view that Proctor later does that which he believes to be good and yet he is hanged. From a religious standpoint, though, one could interpret the quote as being correct, if in fact Proctor's soul was saved.

8. Of what does Giles accuse Putnam?
    He accuses him of killing his neighbors for their land. (If a person were hanged as a witch, his or her land would go up for auction. Putnam was the only man with enough money to buy up all the land.)

9. What is Hale's problem as Proctor and his friends present evidence to Danforth?
    Hale begins to realize that Proctor and his friends have a valid point and that the people who had been accused and sentenced so far could very well have been innocent.

10. Hawthorne thinks of a test for Mary. What is it? Can she do it? Why or why not? He asks Mary to faint, as she fainted in the courtroom. No, she can't do it in front of Hawthorne on demand. She says that she was able to in the courtroom because the mood was set and she got caught up in the mood with the other girls, which enabled her to do it there.

11. Proctor calls Abigail a whore, and he confesses his lechery. Danforth tests Proctor's statement by calling for Elizabeth and asking her why Abigail was dismissed. What does Elizabeth say?
    She lies to protect John.

12. What do the girls do to Mary? What is her response?

    They pretend that her spirit is coming to get them, that she is herself doing some bewitching. Mary tells them to stop it, but when they don't, she ends up breaking down and joining them (for her own protection).

13. What happens to Proctor?

    He is jailed for his contempt of the court and his suspicious activities.

14. What does Hale do?

    He quits the court.

Act Four

1. What explanation does Cheever give for Parris' "mad look"?

    He thinks it is caused by the cows. In other words, the cows are left wandering since their masters are in jail, and there is much contention in the town about ownership and the whole political scene.

2. What did Abigail do?

    Abigail stole money from Parris and disappeared, reportedly left on a ship.

3. Parris says, "You cannot hang this sort. There is danger for me." What "sort" does he mean, and what is the danger to him?

    Because Proctor, Rebecca, Elizabeth, Martha and others were upstanding citizens, generally respected in the community (as opposed to Sarah Good who was a beggar woman), people were truly doubtful of their connections with the devil. Since Parris was so involved with the prosecution of these individuals, he was beginning to get threats on his life.

4. Explain Danforth's reason that a pardon would not be just.

    If he would pardon the remaining accused, the people who had been hanged would have died in vain, unjustly. Rather than admit that the court could have been wrong and therefore admit the others may have been hanged unjustly, he thought it better to continue hanging people so all accused would get the same treatment from the court. His logic was peculiar to say the least.

5. Why has Hale come back to Salem?

    Hale has come back to Salem to encourage the accused to confess and save their lives (whether they are guilty or not).

6. What does Hale want Elizabeth to do?

    Hale wants Elizabeth to convince Proctor to confess.

7. What happened to Giles?
    Giles was pressed to death during questioning.

8. Proctor says, "My honesty is broke, Elizabeth, I am no good man." Explain.
    At this point, he has decided to confess even though he is not guilty. He is telling a lie to save his own life. That in itself takes away his goodness, his honesty. Besides the fact that lying is a sin, he has broken the code of a man's life. Even non-religious people recognize the importance of honesty to one's character. He has broken this code; he is a sinner, he is a failure as a man.

9. What "confession" did Elizabeth make to John?
    She tells him that after much thought, she feels she is also responsible for his affair with Abigail. She thinks if she had been a better, warmer wife, he would not have been inclined to place his affections elsewhere.

10. What did Proctor do after he signed the confession? Why?
    He held the confession and would not give it up to be publicly posted. He knew he was not guilty and did not want to have his lie used to make other innocent people give up their goodness.

11. "I have given you my soul; leave me my name!" Explain.
    By confessing, Proctor has ruined himself, given up his goodness. His hopes for eternal salvation have been destroyed. Since he shall remain alive on the earth for some time to come, he at least wants to have his good name so his life here will still be good. If he has to suffer eternally, the least they can do is to let his remaining years on earth be bearable.

12. "He have his goodness now. God forbid I take it from him!" What does Elizabeth mean?
    Since Proctor refused to make his confession public, the authorities have decided it will not be accepted. He will hang as if he had not confessed. Proctor regains his goodness by accepting his death by hanging rather than becoming an accomplice to the misguided authorities and by holding to the truth that he was not in partnership with the devil. If she were to convince Proctor to give a public confession (and thereby save his life), Elizabeth would put him back in the situation where his goodness would be lost. Then, the loss of his soul would be at least partly her fault. Besides not wanting that responsibility, she recognized the importance of Proctor's eternal well-being and wished that for him over her own desires.

# MULTIPLE CHOICE STUDY GUIDE/QUIZ QUESTIONS - *The Crucible*

## Act One
True or False?

___ 1. The Puritans came to this country for religious freedom; however, when they got here they persecuted others as they had been persecuted. They turned their colony into a place almost as bad as the place they had left.

___ 2. Being under such strict laws and commandments, the Puritans had to repress a lot of their anger and spirit of revenge towards their neighbors. When the witch hunts started, it was an excellent opportunity for them to "let their hair down" and get revenge on their neighbors for whatever petty squabbles they had been having.

___ 3. Tituba was Proctor's slave woman from Barbados. She went with the girls into the forest and was accused of conjuring spirits, accused of being a witch.

___ 4. Abigail was Parris' daughter. She wanted to take Rebecca's place as John Proctor's wife.

___ 5. Betty was Parris' daughter. In the opening scene, she has had some sort of a fit, and the only explanation the people of Salem can find for her condition is the presence of witchcraft in their village.

___ 6. Mrs. Putnam believed witches put spells on her babies and killed them.

___ 7. Thomas Putnam was a greedy, frustrated, bitter man.

___ 8. Parris was well-liked and in complete control of his congregation.

___ 9. Mary wants Abby to tell the truth about the happenings in the woods.

___ 10. Proctor is a weak man, ill-tempered and full of malice.

___ 11. John Proctor and Abigail had an affair.

___ 12. One sign that Betty was bewitched was that she shrieked and flew around the room praising Satan.

___ 13. Rebecca Nurse was truly good woman, kind and gentle in her manner. Rebecca helped to deliver some of the Putnams' babies.

___ 14. The Nurses were not liked by the Putnams because of some land disputes, and this conflict was somewhat revenged by the Putnams when Ann Putnam accused Rebecca of bewitching her newborn babies (implying she was responsible for their deaths).

*Crucible* Multiple Choice Quiz/Questions Page 2

___ 15. Rebecca cast a spell over Betty.

___ 16. Rebecca believed the girls were bewitched.

___ 17. Proctor doesn't attend church because he is an atheist.

___ 18. Parris wanted the deed to his house, and firewood in addition to his salary as minister (not as a part of it).

___ 19. Putnam was a land-grabbing man who would use devious means to get what he wants.

___ 20. Rev. John Hale has come to Salem to take Parris'ss place.

___ 21. Tituba confessed that she had conjured spirits and met with the devil and signed his book.

___ 22. The girls admitted that they were bewitched, and they started naming the names of people they had seen with the devil.

*Crucible* Multiple Choice Quiz/Questions Page 3

Act Two
1. Where does Elizabeth want John to go, and what does she want him to do there?
    a. She wants him to go apologize to Abigail.
    b. She wants him to go help Parris with Betty.
    c. She wants him to go into Salem to tell the authorities that the girls are lying.
    d. She wants him to go convince Tituba to make the girls tell the truth.

2. What is John's response to her prodding?
    a. He is reluctant to go.
    b. He goes right away.
    c. He ignores her.
    d. He tells her to mind her own business.

3. What gift did Mary give Elizabeth?
    a. A Bible
    b. A doll
    c. A basket of flowers
    d. a & b

4. What was the "evidence" against Sarah Good?
    a. She confessed to witchcraft.
    b. She mumbled after begging for cider and bread
    c. She could not recite the commandments in court.
    d. All of the above

5. Why doesn't Proctor want Mary to go back to court?
    a. If she goes back, that makes him further involved.
    b. He believes that the accusations are false and the girls are frauds.
    c. It isn't a just court in Proctor's eyes.
    d. All of the above

6. Why does Elizabeth think Abigail wants to kill her?
    a. She is sick and a little paranoid.
    b. She believes that Abby wants to take her place as John's wife.
    c. She believes Abby is bewitched and will try to destroy anything good.
    d. a & c

*Crucible* Multiple Choice Quiz/Questions Page 4

7. Why did Hale come to Proctor's house?
    a. He wanted to find out why Parris was so bitter.
    b. He wanted to question them prior to seeing them in court.
    c. He wanted to find out if the rumor about John and Abby was true.
    d. All of the above

8. What things are "suspicious" about Proctor and his family?
    a. Proctor does not go to church regularly.
    b. The youngest son has not been baptized.
    c. He could not remember all of the commandments.
    d. All of the above

9. Hale asks Elizabeth if she believes in witches. What is her reply?
    a. If she is accused of being a witch, she cannot believe in witches.
    b. If the Bible says that witches exist, she cannot dispute the Bible.
    c. She does not believe the girls are telling the truth.
    d. a & b

10. On what charge(s) was Rebecca Nurse arrested?
    a. The murder of Goody Putnam's babies
    b. Impious conduct
    c. Conduct unbefitting a Puritan woman
    d. Inability to say the ten commandments from memory

11. Why does Cheever come to the Proctor house?
    a. He comes to question John.
    b. He comes to arrest Elizabeth.
    c. He comes to talk with John about what to do about Parris
    d. He comes to ask John's opinion about whether the girls are lying.

12. What is the deciding factor in Elizabeth's arrest?
    a. Her inability to recite the ten commandments
    b. Her possession of the doll with a needle in it
    c. The fact that she has not had her son baptized
    d. Abby's testimony

*Crucible* Multiple Choice Quiz/Questions Page 5

13. What will happen to Proctor if he tries to discredit Abby?
    a. She will tell that they had an affair.
    b. She will claim she has seen him with the devil.
    c. She will bewitch Elizabeth.
    d. She will end their affair.

14. Why doesn't Mary want to testify about the doll?
    a. She doesn't want to get involved.
    b. She is afraid of Abigail.
    c. She is afraid of the devil.
    d. She thinks she will look like a fool.

*Crucible* Multiple Choice Quiz/Questions Page 6

Act Three
1. Why do Giles and Francis want to see Danforth?
    a. They intend to beat him to his senses.
    b. They want to explain their roles in the witchcraft scheme.
    c. They want to persuade the judge that their wives are good women.
    d. They want to explain how Parris is at fault.

2. What is Parris' argument against Proctor?
    a. Parris says that Proctor is trying to overthrow the court.
    b. Parris says that Proctor is biased because of his position between Abigail and Elizabeth.
    c. Parris says that Proctor is just getting even with him.
    d. b & c

3. What does Mary tell Danforth?
    a. Abigail is not evil; she's just in love with Proctor.
    b. The girls have been lying.
    c. Tituba was responsible for their actions in the woods.
    d. Abigail gave Elizabeth the doll.

4. Why did Danforth grant Elizabeth extra time?
    a. He didn't blame her for being jealous of Abigail.
    b. She was trying to convince John to confess.
    c. She said she was pregnant.
    d. He almost believed Mary's story.

5. What did the paper that ninety-one people signed say?
    a. The community wanted Parris removed from service as their minister.
    b. Rebecca, Elizabeth and Martha were all good, upstanding, God-loving citizens.
    c. John and Elizabeth should be released.
    d. all of the above

6. What quote did Proctor use to help Mary remain brave?
    a. "Truth is always best."
    b. "God helps those who help themselves."
    c. "Do that which is good, and no harm will come to thee."
    d. The twenty-third Psalm

*Crucible* Multiple Choice Quiz/Questions Page 7

7. Of what does Giles accuse Putnam?
    a. He accuses him of killing his neighbors for their land.
    b. He accuses him of being in service to the devil.
    c. He accuses him of taking advantage of the girls.
    d. He accuses him of being a hypocrite.

8. What is Hale's problem as Proctor and his friends present evidence to Danforth?
    a. He worries about his own safety from the girls' accusations.
    b. He sees that he has been a failure at removing witchcraft from Salem.
    c. He thinks his reputation will be hurt.
    d. He begins to realize that the people who had been accused and sentenced so far could very well have been innocent.

9. Hawthorne thinks of a test for Mary. What is it?
    a. He asks her to recite the ten commandments.
    b. He asks her to faint, as she fainted in the courtroom.
    c. He asks her to fly around the room.
    d. He asks her to stick a pin in her poppet.

10. When asked why Abigail was released from her service, what did Elizabeth respond?
    a. She was dissatisfied with Abigail.
    b. She, in her sickness, thought Abigail and John fancied each other.
    c. John was not a lecher.
    d. All of the above

11. What do the girls do to Mary?
    a. They glare at her.
    b. They threaten her, saying she will regret her wrongful accusations about them for the rest of her life.
    c. They pretend that her spirit is coming to get them.
    d. They pretend the devil is in the room.

12. What happens to Proctor?
    a. He is jailed for being a lecher.
    b. He is jailed for lying to the court.
    c. He is jailed for adultery.
    d. He is jailed for his contempt of the court and his suspicious activities.

*Crucible* Multiple Choice Quiz/Questions Page 8

Act Four
1. What explanation does Cheever give for Parris' "mad look"?
    a. Parris is at his wits' end wondering what to do with Abigail.
    b. The devil has run rampant in Salem, Parris'ss parish.
    c. Parris is under a spell.
    d. He thinks it is caused by the cows.

2. What did Abigail do?
    a. Abigail stole money from Parris and disappeared.
    b. Abigail killed herself.
    c. Abigail begged for everyone's forgiveness.
    d. Abigail confessed that she and the others had been lying.

3. Identify the speaker: "You cannot hang this sort. There is danger for me."
    a. Proctor
    b. Danforth
    c. Hale
    d. Parris

4. Explain Danforth's reason that a pardon would not be a good idea.
    a. If he would pardon the remaining accused, the people who had been hanged would have died in vain.
    b. Rather than admit that the court could have been wrong and therefore admit the others may have been hanged unjustly, he thought it better to continue hanging people so all accused would get the same treatment from the court.
    c. The citizens would lose respect for the court and anarchy would prevail.
    d. a & b

5. Why has Hale come back to Salem?
    a. To free the unjustly jailed
    b. To encourage the accused to confess and save their lives
    c. To discredit the girls
    d. All of the above

6. What does Hale want Elizabeth to do?
    a. Confess to save her baby
    b. Repent
    c. Convince Proctor to confess
    d. Forgive Abigail

*Crucible* Multiple Choice Quiz/Questions Page 9

7. What happened to Giles?
    a. Giles was pressed to death during questioning.
    b. He was hanged.
    c. He was released.
    d. He escaped and went to live in another village.

8. What "confession" did Elizabeth make to John?
    a. She has been involved with witchcraft.
    b. She also had an affair.
    c. She secretly hoped Abigail would be killed by an angry mob.
    d. She feels she is also responsible for his affair with Abigail.

9. What did Proctor do after he signed the confession?
    a. He collapsed, a broken man.
    b. He tore it up.
    c. He begged Elizabeth to forgive him.
    d. a & c

# ANSWER KEY - MULTIPLE CHOICE STUDY/QUIZ QUESTIONS
## *The Crucible*

| Act 1 | Act 2 | Act 3 | Act 4 |
|---|---|---|---|
| 1. True | 1. C | 1. C | 1. D |
| 2. True | 2. A | 2. A | 2. A |
| 3. False | 3. B | 3. B | 3. D |
| 4. False | 4. D | 4. C | 4. D |
| 5. True | 5. D | 5. B | 5. B |
| 6. True | 6. B | 6. C | 6. C |
| 7. True | 7. B | 7. A | 7. A |
| 8. False | 8. D | 8. D | 8. D |
| 9. True | 9. D | 9. B | 9. B |
| 10. False | 10. A | 10. D | |
| 11. True | 11. B | 11. C | |
| 12. False | 12. B | 12. D | |
| 13. True | 13. A | | |
| 14. True | 14. B | | |
| 15. False | | | |
| 16. False | | | |
| 17. False | | | |
| 18. True | | | |
| 19. True | | | |
| 20. False | | | |
| 21. True | | | |
| 22. True | | | |

# PREREADING VOCABULARY WORKSHEETS

# VOCABULARY - *The Crucible*

<u>Reading Assignment 1</u> Part I: Using Prior Knowledge and Contextual Clues
    Below are the sentences in which the vocabulary words appear in the text. Read the sentence. Use any clues you can find in the sentence combined with your prior knowledge, and write what you think the underlined words mean in the space provided.

1. But we never <u>conjured</u> spirits.

2. There is a <u>faction</u> that is sworn to drive me from my pulpit. Do you understand that?

3. <u>Abominations</u> are done in the forest--

4. But Betty collapses in her hands and lies <u>inert</u> on the bed.

5. He need not have been a <u>partisan</u> of any faction in the town, but there is evidence to suggest that he had a sharp and biting way with <u>hypocrites</u>.

6. In Proctor's presence a fool felt his foolishness instantly -- and a Proctor is always marked for <u>calumny</u> therefore.

7. That is a notorious sign of witchcraft afoot, Goody Nurse, a <u>prodigious</u> sign!

8. It's somewhat true; there are many that <u>quail</u> to bring their children--

9. Why, we are surely gone wild this year. What <u>anarchy</u> is this?

*Crucible* Reading Assignment 1 Vocabulary Continued

Part II: Determining the Meaning
    Match the vocabulary words to their dictionary definitions.

___ 1. conjured           A. to lose courage; decline; fail; give way
___ 2. faction             B. unable to move or act
___ 3. abominations     C. summoned by oath or spell
___ 4. inert                D. false statements knowingly made to injure someone
___ 5. hypocrites       E. small group, usually contentious, within a larger group
___ 6. partisan          F. people who say they believe one way, but whose actions show they believe another
___ 7. calumny          G. political disorder and confusion
___ 8. prodigious       H. things that elicit great dislike or abhorrence
___ 9. quail               I. extraordinary; marvelous
___ 10. anarchy         J. militant supporter of a party, cause, faction or idea

# VOCABULARY - *The Crucible*

Reading Assignment 2  Part I: Using Prior Knowledge and Contextual Clues
    Below are the sentences in which the vocabulary words appear in the text. Read the sentence. Use any clues you can find in the sentence combined with your prior knowledge, and write what you think the underlined words mean in the space provided.

1. This is a beloved errand for him; on being called here to <u>ascertain</u> witchcraft he felt the pride of the specialist whose unique knowledge has at least been publicly called for.


2. Evidently we are not quite certain even now whether <u>diabolism</u> is holy and not to be scoffed at.


3. And it is no accident that we should be so <u>bemused</u>.


4. . . . he is called up and damned not only by our social <u>antagonists</u> but by our own side, whatever it may be.


5. I have no doubt that people *were* communing with, and even worshiping, the Devil in Salem, and if the whole truth could be known in this case, as it is in others, we should discover a regular and conventionalized <u>propitiation</u> of the dark spirit.


6. How could it be the Devil? Why would he choose my house to strike? We have all manner of <u>licentious</u> people right here in the village!


7. You cannot <u>evade</u> me, Abigail. Did your cousin drink any of the brew in that kettle?


8. On their <u>ecstatic</u> cries, the curtain falls.

*Crucible* Reading Assignment 2 Vocabulary Continued

Part II: Determining the Meaning
Match the vocabulary words to their dictionary definitions. If there are words for which you cannot figure out the definition by contextual clues and by process of elimination, look them up in a dictionary.

___ 11. ascertain
___ 12. diabolism
___ 13. bemused
___ 14. antagonists
___ 15. propitiation
___ 16. licentious
___ 17. evade
___ 18. ecstatic

A. appeasement
B. in a state of exalted delight
C. find out; detect
D. having no regard for accepted rules or standards
E. witchcraft; sorcery
F. escape or avoid by cleverness or deceit
G. confused
H. adversaries; opponents

VOCABULARY - *The Crucible*

Reading Assignment 3    Part I: Using Prior Knowledge and Contextual Clues
   Below are the sentences in which the vocabulary words appear in the text. Read the sentence. Use any clues you can find in the sentence combined with your prior knowledge, and write what you think the underlined words mean in the space provided.

1. Proctor, holding back a full condemnation of her: It is a fault, it is a fault, Elizabeth--you're the mistress here, not Mary Warren.

2. I am only wondering how I may prove what she told me, Elizabeth. If the girl's a saint now, I think it is not easy to prove she's fraud, and the town gone so silly.

3. Her strangeness throws him off, and her evident pallor and weakness.

4. Elizabeth, perplexed, looking at the doll: Why, thank you, it's a fair poppet.

5. Mary Warren, with an indignant edge: She tried to kill me many times, Goody Proctor!

6. Aye, but then Judge Hawthorne say, "Recite for us your commandments!"--leaning avidly toward them--and all of the ten she could not say a single one.

7. I only hope you'll not be so sarcastical no more. . . . I--I would have you speak civilly to me, from this out.

8. Woman, am I so base? Do you truly think me base?

*Crucible* Reading Assignment 3 Vocabulary Continued

Part II: Determining the Meaning
    Match the vocabulary words to their dictionary definitions.

___ 19. condemnation      A. bewildered; puzzled; confused
___ 20. fraud      B. expressing mocking or contemptuous remarks
___ 21. pallor      C. severe reproof; strong censure
___ 22. perplexed      D. having low moral standards; contemptible; inferior
___ 23. indignant      E. enthusiastically
___ 24. avidly      F. deliberate deception for unfair or unlawful gains
___ 25. sarcastical      G. extreme paleness
___ 26. base      H. filled with an anger aroused by something unjust or unworthy

# VOCABULARY - *The Crucible*

<u>Reading Assignment 4</u>   Part I: Using Prior Knowledge and Contextual Clues

Below are the sentences in which the vocabulary words appear in the text. Read the sentence. Use any clues you can find in the sentence combined with your prior knowledge, and write what you think the underlined words mean in the space provided.

1. Believe me, Mr. Nurse, if Rebecca Nurse be <u>tainted</u>, then nothing's left to stop the whole green world from burning.

2. Cheever, <u>ineptly</u> reaching toward Elizabeth . . .

3. I had my doubts, Proctor, I had my doubts, but here's <u>calamity</u>, *To Hale, showing the needle:* You see it, sir, it is a needle!

4. Were there murder done, perhaps, and never brought to light? Abomination? Some secret <u>blasphemy</u> that stinks to Heaven? Think on cause, man, and let you help me to discover it.

5. Proctor, *moving <u>menacingly</u> toward her:* You will tell the court how that poppet came here and who stuck the needle in.

6. Abby'll charge <u>lechery</u> on you, Mr. Proctor!

7. It is a <u>providence</u>, and no great change; we are only what we always were, but naked now.

*Crucible* Reading Assignment 4 Vocabulary Continued

Part II: Determining the Meaning
    Match the vocabulary words to their dictionary definitions.

___ 27. tainted              A. disaster
___ 28. ineptly              B. promiscuity
___ 29. calamity             C. having a moral defect; infected
___ 30. blasphemy            D. awkwardly
___ 31. menacingly           E. work of divine direction
___ 32. lechery              F. an irreverent or impious act or utterance
___ 33. providence           G. threateningly

# VOCABULARY - *The Crucible*

## Reading Assignment 5

Part I: Using Prior Knowledge and Contextual Clues

Below are the sentences in which the vocabulary words appear in the text. Read the sentence. Use any clues you can find in the sentence combined with your prior knowledge, and write what you think the underlined words mean in the space provided.

1. How do you dare come roarin' into this court! Are you gone daft, Corey?

2. Giles Corey, sir, and a more contentious--

3. And how do you imagine to help her cause with such contemptuous riot? Now be gone.

4. Mary Warren, *hardly audible:* Aye.

5. But if he hide in anonymity I must know why. Now sir, the government and central church demand of you the name of him who reported Mr. Thomas Putnam a common murderer.

6. This is a court of law, Mister. I'll have no effrontery here!

7. . . . I dare not take a life without there be a proof so immaculate no slightest qualm of conscience may doubt it.

*Crucible* Reading Assignment 5 Vocabulary Continued

Part II: Determining the Meaning
    Match the vocabulary words to their dictionary definitions.

    ___ 34. daft                A. quarrelsome
    ___ 35. contentious         B. audacity; insulting boldness
    ___ 36. contemptuous        C. a sensation of misgiving or uneasiness
    ___ 37. audible             D. crazy; foolish; stupid
    ___ 38. anonymity           E. able to be heard
    ___ 39. effrontery          F. scornful; disdainful
    ___ 40. qualm               G. secrecy; having an unknown or unacknowledged name

# VOCABULARY - *The Crucible*

Reading Assignment 6  Part I: Using Prior Knowledge and Contextual Clues

Below are the sentences in which the vocabulary words appear in the text. Read the sentence. Use any clues you can find in the sentence combined with your prior knowledge, and write what you think the underlined words mean.

1. In which she swears that she never saw familiar spirits, apparitions, nor any manifest of the Devil.

2. He charges contemplation of murder.

3. She glances at Abigail, who is staring down at her remorselessly.

4. That were pretense, sir.

5. She is transfixed--with all the girls, she is whimpering open-mouthed, agape at the ceiling.

6. Will you confess yourself befouled with Hell, or do you keep that black allegiance yet?

Part II: Determining the Meaning

Match the vocabulary words to their dictionary definitions.

___ 41. manifest  
___ 42. remorselessly  
___ 43. contemplation  
___ 44. pretense  
___ 45. transfixed  
___ 46. allegiance  

A. the act of pretending  
B. loyalty  
C. something apparent to the sight or understanding  
D. thoughtful observation or meditation  
E. mercilessly; having no pity or compassion  
F. rendered motionless with terror, amazement or awe

# VOCABULARY - *The Crucible*

<u>Reading Assignment 7</u>  Part I: Using Prior Knowledge and Contextual Clues

Below are the sentences in which the vocabulary words appear in the text. Read the sentence. Use any clues you can find in the sentence combined with your prior knowledge, and write what you think the underlined words mean in the space provided.

1. Now hear me, and beguile yourselves no more.


2. . . . reprieve or pardon must cast doubt upon the guilt of them that died till now.


3. If retaliation is your fear, know this--I should hang ten thousand that dared to rise against the law, and an ocean of salt tears could not melt the resolution of the statutes.


4. Is he yet adamant?


5. Giles is dead. *He looks at her incredulously.*


6. He would not answer aye or nay to his indictment; for if he denied the charge they's hang him surely, and auction out his property. So he stand mute, and died Christian under the law.


7. I have confessed myself! Is there no good penitence but it be public?

*Crucible* Reading Assignment 7 Vocabulary Continued

Part II: Determining the Meaning
   Match the vocabulary words to their dictionary definitions.

___ 47. beguile          A. statement of criminal charges
___ 48. reprieve         B. a law, decree or edict
___ 49. statutes         C. performing of penance
___ 50. adamant          D. disbelievingly
___ 51. incredulously    E. postponement of punishment
___ 52. indictment       F. firm in purpose or opinion; unyielding
___ 53. penitence        G. delude; cheat; divert

# ANSWER KEY: VOCABULARY *The Crucible*

**Assignment 1**
1. C
2. E
3. H
4. B
5. F
6. J
7. D
8. I
9. A
10. G

**Assignment 2**
11. C
12. E
13. G
14. H
15. A
16. D
17. F
18. B

**Assignment 3**
19. C
20. F
21. G
22. A
23. H
24. E
25. B
26. D

**Assignment 4**
27. C
28. D
29. A
30. F
31. G
32. B
33. E

**Assignment 5**
34. D
35. A
36. F
37. E
38. G
39. B
40. C

**Assignment 6**
41. C
42. E
43. D
44. A
45. F
46. B

**Assignment 7**
47. G
48. E
49. B
50. F
51. D
52. A
53. C

# DAILY LESSONS

# LESSON ONE

Objectives
    1. To introduce the *Crucible* unit
    2. To distribute plays and other related materials
    3. To preview the study questions for Act One
    4. To familiarize students with the vocabulary for Act One

NOTES: Prior to this lesson you need to assign students to bring in one article about or related to either witchcraft or Puritanism. Prepare a bulletin board with background paper and the title: THE CRUCIBLE: A PURITAN WITCH HUNT.

    The reading of *The Crucible* is all done orally because it is a play. If you wish to make a complete production of this play, insert several days of preparation for part assignments, practice, staging, and set creation at the beginning of the unit. This makes a good class project; little scenery and few props are necessary.

Activity #1
    Have students each stand up and give a summary of the articles they have brought relating to witchcraft or Puritanism. It would probably be best to have all reports on one topic and then all the reports on the other. Have students post their articles on the bulletin board you have prepared. Use these article reports as a springboard for discussion about the Puritans and witchcraft.

Transition: The play you are about to read, *The Crucible*, is the story of the witch hunt that took place in the Puritan village of Salem, Massachusetts in the early 1600's.

Activity #2
    Distribute the materials students will use in this unit. Explain in detail how students are to use these materials.

    Study Guides  Students should read the study guide questions for each reading assignment prior to beginning the reading assignment to get a feeling for what events and ideas are important in the section they are about to read. After reading the section, students will (as a class or individually) answer the questions to review the important events and ideas from that section of the play. Students should keep the study guides as study materials for the unit test.

    Vocabulary  Prior to reading a reading assignment, students will do vocabulary work related to the section of the play they are about to read. Following the completion of the reading of the play, there will be a vocabulary review of all the words used in the vocabulary assignments. Students should keep their vocabulary work as study materials for the unit test.

Reading Assignment Sheet  You need to fill in the reading assignment sheet to let students know by when their reading has to be completed. You can either write the assignment sheet up on a side blackboard or bulletin board and leave it there for students to see each day, or you can "ditto" copies for each student to have. In either case, you should advise students to become very familiar with the reading assignments so they know what is expected of them.

Extra Activities Center  The Extra Activities Packet portion of this unit contains suggestions for an extra library of related books and articles in your classroom as well as crossword and word search puzzles. Make an extra activities center in your room where you will keep these materials for students to use. (Bring the play and articles in from the library and keep several copies of the puzzles on hand.) Explain to students that these materials are available for students to use when they finish reading assignments or other class work early.

Nonfiction Assignment Sheet  Explain to students that they each are to read at least one non-fiction piece from the in-class library at some time during the unit. Students will fill out a nonfiction assignment sheet after completing the reading to help you evaluate their reading experiences) and to help the students think about and evaluate their own reading experiences.

Books  Each school has its own rules and regulations regarding student use of school books. Advise students of the procedures that are normal for your school.


Activity #3
Preview the study questions and have students do the vocabulary work for Act One of *The Crucible*. If students do not finish this assignment during this class period, they should complete it prior to the next class meeting.

# NONFICTION ASSIGNMENT SHEET
(To be completed after reading the required nonfiction article)

Name _____ Date _____

Title of Nonfiction Read _____

Written By _____ Publication Date _____

I. Factual Summary: Write a short summary of the piece you read.



II. Vocabulary
    1. With which vocabulary words in the piece did you encounter some degree of difficulty?



    2. How did you resolve your lack of understanding with these words?

III. Interpretation: What was the main point the author wanted you to get from reading his work?

IV. Criticism
    1. With which points of the piece did you agree or find easy to accept? Why?



    2. With which points of the piece did you disagree or find difficult to believe? Why?

V. Personal Response: What do you think about this piece? OR How does this piece influence your ideas?

# LESSON TWO

## Objectives
1. To begin reading *The Crucible* out loud in class
2. To give students practice reading orally
3. To evaluate students' oral reading

NOTE: If you have not yet evaluated your students oral reading for this marking period, this is an excellent chance to do so. An oral reading evaluation form is provided for your convenience following this lesson.

Parts To Be Spoken In This Session:

Narrator (stage descriptions and directions; italicized)
Miller's voice (background information; non-italics, non-character passages)

| | |
|---|---|
| Tituba | Rebecca Nurse |
| Parris | Giles |
| Abigail | Proctor |
| Susanna | Betty |
| Mrs. Putnam | Mary Warren |
| Mr. Putnam | Mercy Lewis |

## Activity

Assign the above parts to various students in your class. Read the first act up to Hale's entrance where the text says, "He appears loaded down with half a dozen heavy books." If you do not reach this point during the class period, students should read to there on their own prior to the next class period.

## ORAL READING EVALUATION - *The Crucible*

Name _____ Class _____ Date _____

| SKILL | EXCELLENT | GOOD | AVERAGE | FAIR | POOR |
|---|---|---|---|---|---|
| Fluency | 5 | 4 | 3 | 2 | 1 |
| Clarity | 5 | 4 | 3 | 2 | 1 |
| Audibility | 5 | 4 | 3 | 2 | 1 |
| Pronunciation | 5 | 4 | 3 | 2 | 1 |
| _____ | 5 | 4 | 3 | 2 | 1 |
| _____ | 5 | 4 | 3 | 2 | 1 |

Total _____ Grade _____

Comments:

## LESSON THREE

Objectives
1. To complete reading Act One of *The Crucible*
2. To review the main ideas and events of Act One

Parts To Be Spoken In This Session

| | |
|---|---|
| Narrator | Betty |
| Miller's voice | Tituba |
| Hale | Abigail |
| Parris | Proctor |
| Rebecca | Giles Corey |
| Putnam | Mrs. Putnam |

Activity #1

Assign various students the speaking parts noted above. Complete reading Act One.

Activity #2

Discuss the study guide questions for Act One in detail. Write the "answers" on the board or overhead projector for students to copy down for study use later.

TEACHER'S NOTE: Depending on the students, I have let different students write the answers on the board or even ask the questions to lead the group. I would then jump in as necessary to guide the discussion. Use whatever techniques your particular students will handle best.

# LESSON FOUR

Objectives
1. To begin reading Act Two of *The Crucible* out loud in class
2. To give students practice reading orally
3. To preview the study questions for Act Two
4. To familiarize students with the vocabulary for Act Two

Parts To Be Spoken In This Session:
Narrator (stage descriptions and directions; italicized)
Elizabeth
Proctor
Mary Warren
Hale

Activity #1
Give students ten to fifteen minutes at the beginning of the class period to do the prereading work for Act Two.

Activity #2
Assign the above parts to various students in your class. Read the second act up to Giles' entrance. At Hale's entrance, you may wish to change the "actor" for Proctor's part, to give someone else a chance to read. If you don't finish reading to Giles' entrance during the class period, students should read to there on their own prior to the next class period.

# LESSON FIVE

Objectives
   1. To complete reading Act Two of *The Crucible*
   2. To review the main ideas and events of Act Two
   3. To preview the study questions for Act Three
   4. To familiarize students with the vocabulary in Act Three

Parts To Be Spoken In This Session:
   Narrator          Elizabeth
   Giles             Hale
   Proctor           Cheever
   Francis Nurse     Mary Warren

Activity #1
   Assign various students the speaking parts noted above. Complete reading Act Two orally.

Activity #2
   Discuss the study guide questions for Act Two in detail. Write the "answers" on the board for students to copy down for study use later.

Activity #3
   Tell students that prior to the next class period they should complete the prereading work for Act Three.

# LESSON SIX

Objectives
1. To begin reading Act Three of *The Crucible* out loud in class
2. To give students practice reading orally

Parts To Be Spoken In This Session:
Narrator (stage descriptions and directions; italicized)
Hawthorne
Martha Corey
Danforth
Giles
Herrick
Hale
Parris
Francis

Activity
Assign the above parts to various students in your class. Read the third act up to the entrance of Susanna, Mercy, Betty and Abigail. When Proctor hands Danforth the first paper, you may wish to appoint a new Danforth to give another student a chance to read. If you don't finish reading to the girls' entrance during the class period, students should read to there on their own prior to the next class period.

# LESSON SEVEN

## Objectives
1. To complete reading Act Three of *The Crucible*
2. To review the main ideas and events of Act Three
3. To preview the study questions for Act Four
4. To familiarize students with the vocabulary in Act Four

Parts To Be Spoken In This Session:

| | |
|---|---|
| Narrator | Giles |
| Abigail | Mercy |
| Susanna | Francis |
| Cheever | Danforth |
| Mary | Proctor |
| Hawthorne | Parris |
| Elizabeth | |

## Activity #1
Assign various students the speaking parts noted above. Complete reading Act Three orally.

## Activity #2
Discuss the study guide questions for Act Three in detail. Write the "answers" on the board or overhead projector for students to copy down for study use later.

## Activity #3
Tell students that prior to the next class period they should complete the prereading work for Act Four.

# LESSON EIGHT

Objectives
1. To read Act Four of *The Crucible* out loud in class
2. To give students practice reading orally

Parts To Be Spoken In This Session:
Narrator (stage descriptions and directions; italicized)
Herrick              Rebecca
Tituba               Proctor
Sarah Good           Elizabeth
Hopkins              Hale
Danforth             Parris
Hawthorne

Activity

Assign the above parts to various students in your class. Read the fourth act. If you do not finish during the class period, students should complete reading the play on their own prior to the next class period.

# LESSON NINE

Objectives
1. To review the main ideas and events of Act Four
2. To review all of the vocabulary work done in this unit

Activity #1

Discuss the answers for the study guide questions in detail. Write the answers down on the board or overhead projector for students to copy for study use.

Activity #2

Choose one (or more) of the vocabulary review activities that follow and spend your class period as directed in the activity. Some of the materials for these review activities are located in the Vocabulary Resources section of this unit.

# VOCABULARY REVIEW ACTIVITIES

1. Divide your class into two teams and have an old-fashioned spelling or definition bee.

2. Give each of your students (or students in groups of two, three or four) a *The Crucible* Vocabulary Word Search Puzzle. The person (group) to find all of the vocabulary words in the puzzle first wins.

3. Give students a *The Crucible* Vocabulary Word Search Puzzle without the word list. The person or group to find the most vocabulary words in the puzzle wins.

4. Use a *The Crucible* Vocabulary Crossword Puzzle. Put the puzzle onto a transparency on the overhead projector (so everyone can see it), and do the puzzle together as a class.

5. Give students a *The Crucible* Vocabulary Matching Worksheet to do.

6. Divide your class into two teams. Use the *Crucible* vocabulary words with their letters jumbled as a word list. Student 1 from Team A faces off against Student 1 from Team B. You write the first jumbled word on the board. The first student (1A or 1B) to unscramble the word wins the chance for his/her team to score points. If 1A wins the jumble, go to student 2A and give him/her a definition. He/she must give you the correct spelling of the vocabulary word which fits that definition. If he/she does, Team A scores a point, and you give student 3A a definition for which you expect a correctly spelled matching vocabulary word. Continue giving Team A definitions until some team member makes an incorrect response. An incorrect response sends the game back to the jumbled-word face off, this time with students 2A and 2B. Instead of repeating giving definitions to the first few students of each team, continue with the student after the one who gave the last incorrect response on the team. For example, if Team B wins the jumbled-word face-off, and student 5B gave the last incorrect answer for Team B, you would start this round of definition questions with student 6B, and so on. The team with the most points wins!

7. Have students write a story in which they correctly use as many vocabulary words as possible. Have students read their compositions orally! Post the most original compositions on your bulletin board!

# LESSON TEN

## Objectives
1. To study the play more closely through all four acts
2. To give students the opportunity to practice their personal interaction skills in a small group setting
3. To give students the opportunity to practice their public speaking skills as they report their small group findings

## Activity #1
Divide the class into five groups. Each group should be assigned one of the following:

1. How does the play show the conflict of the individual vs. society?
2. How was Puritanism a motivating force in the witch hunt?
3. What are the conflicts between the characters (specifically Nurse/Putnam, Parris/Proctor, Putnam/Proctor, Proctor/Hale, Proctor/Elizabeth, Proctor/Abigail, and Abigail/Elizabeth)?
4. What motivates Abigail and the girls?
5. What is the effect of confession in the play, specifically John to Elizabeth, Elizabeth to John, Abigail to Parris, Mary to Danforth, Tituba to Hale, other accused to the court, John to Danforth?

Students within the group will each take approximately one act of the play and find all the references to their group's topic in that chapter. (If the groups have more than four people, have more than one student work on the same act. If the groups have less than four people, the group members will have to cover more than one act.) Students should jot down their findings.

When the individuals are done with their research, group members should get together to discuss their findings. Based on their research, they should try to draw some conclusions about the topic.

## Activity #2
The groups will each report their findings and conclusions to the whole class. One student for each group should be appointed "spokesperson" to give the group's findings and conclusions.

The teacher or a student should write down on the board or overhead all of the findings and conclusions.

# LESSON ELEVEN

## Objectives
1. To conclude the theme reports and discussion from Lesson Ten
2. To give students time to clean up & check their notes and to work on the nonfiction reading assignment

## Activity #1
Continue any reports and discussion not completed in Lesson Ten. Be sure to continue writing down all important information for students to copy into their notes for study use later.

## Activity #2
If you still have time remaining after completing the discussions, give students time to compare, correct and revise their notes and/or time to work on their nonfiction reading assignments. If you are certain that you will definitely have time left over, have made arrangements for your class to go to the library to get suitable reading material either for their personal reading enjoyment or for their nonfiction reading assignment.


# LESSON TWELVE

## Objectives
1. To give students the opportunity to practice writing to inform
2. To give students the chance to think in detail about at least one of the themes in *The Crucible*
3. To give the teacher a chance to evaluate students' individual writing
4. To give students the opportunity to correct their writing errors and produce an error-free paper

## Activity
Distribute Writing Assignment #1. Discuss the directions orally in detail. Allow the remaining class time for students to complete the activity.

If students do not have enough class time to finish, the papers may be collected at the beginning of the next class period.

Follow - Up: After you have graded the assignments, have a writing conference with the students. (This unit schedules one in Lesson Eight.) After the writing conference, allow students to revise their papers using your suggestions and corrections. Give them about three days from the date they receive their papers to complete the revision. I suggest grading the revisions on an A-C-E scale (all revisions well-done, some revisions made, few or no revisions made). This will speed your grading time and still give some credit for the students' efforts.

# WRITING ASSIGNMENT #1 - *The Crucible*

## PROMPT

Your assignment is to take the information about one of the ideas we've discussed and form it into a written paper. Your research has been done through group work, reports and discussion. Now, take that information and shape it into an essay.

## PREWRITING

One way to start is to decide which of the five topics we have discussed most interests you. Take a look at your notes and give the topic some more thought. Jot down ideas relevant to your topic. Then, on your scratch paper, pick out your three best points. Organize any other thoughts you've put down to see if they can be used as supporting examples or statements for any of your three main points. Scratch out anything that's left. Now go back and jot down any more ideas you have which will support your three ideas.

## DRAFTING

A diagram of a basic, five-paragraph essay might look like this:
¶1. Introduce essay topic
¶2. Main Idea (topic sentence) followed by examples or details supporting main idea
¶3. Main idea (topic sentence) followed by examples or details supporting main idea
¶4. Main idea (topic sentence) followed by examples or details supporting main idea
¶5. Summary/Closing

Once you have mastered the basic skills of making a main topic, supporting that main topic with main ideas of substance and explaining those main ideas with examples or details, a whole new world of creativity in writing opens up for you. It is then you can perfect your style of writing, choosing a <u>way of delivering</u> your ideas.

## PROMPT

When you finish the rough draft of your paper, ask a student who sits near you to read it. After reading your rough draft, he/she should tell you what he/she liked best about your work, which parts were difficult to understand, and ways in which your work could be improved. Reread your paper considering your critic's comments, and make the corrections you think are necessary.

## PROOFREADING

Do a final proofreading of your paper double-checking your grammar, spelling, organization, and the clarity of your ideas.

# LESSON THIRTEEN

Objectives
- 1. To give students the opportunity to do some creative writing
- 2. To give students practice cooperating and compromising
- 3. To reexamine the facts of *The Crucible* in a slightly different way
- 4. To consider the facts, motives, actions, and reactions in the play

Explain to students that in the next couple of class periods you will be putting Abigail Williams on trial for the murder of the people of Salem who were hanged (or otherwise died) as a result of the Salem witch hunt. Putting Abigail on trial will involve three stages of work: preparation (deciding who will take part in the trial--the characters needed), writing (deciding what arguments will be used on both sides of the case, deciding what questions will be used in the trial and what the likely responses will be to the questions asked), and actually performing the trial and coming to a verdict.

Activity #1

The first thing students should do is to (as a group) decide who will take part in the trial. Write a list of the characters they think they will need to use for the trial. Be sure they remember to pick a judge and a jury, a prosecuting attorney and a defense attorney in addition to other characters and witnesses. Assign these parts to various students in your class.

Activity #2

The next thing students should do is to work out the dialogue and staging for their trial scene. This can be done in several ways. One way is to have students interact as the characters they have been assigned and to tape record or write down the dialogue they use. Another way is to have students as a class figure out the best dialogue possible, and then write that down or tape record it. Probably the best way to handle this group writing assignment is to start with the latter way and then fill it in using the first way. In other words, start with having students figure out the best basic arguments to use on both sides of the case and the general scenario for the scene, and then let students role-play and improvise to create the actual dialogue.

# LESSON FOURTEEN

Objectives
    1. To complete the group writing assignment from Lesson Thirteen
    2. To act out the scene written in the group writing assignment
    3. To come to a verdict about Abigail's guilt or innocence

Activity #1
    If your students need more time to complete writing the scene for Abigail's trial, give them the time they need at the beginning of this period. (Some classes may even need this entire period, in which case you will need to insert another lesson for the acting out of the scene.)

Activity #2
    Give students this class period to act out Abigail's trial scene. Following the conclusion of the scene, the jury should reach a verdict and the judge should impose a sentence. Have your class discuss what sentence would be appropriate to give Abigail if she is found guilty.

# LESSON FIFTEEN

Objectives
    1. To evaluate students' writing
    2. To have students revise their Writing Assignment 1 papers
    3. To have students write a descriptive essay in a letter format
    4. To give students an opportunity to produce an error-free paper and to apply the teacher's suggestions
    5. To evaluate students understanding the material covered so far

Activity #1
    Distribute Writing Assignment 2 and discuss the directions in detail.
Give students this class period to work on this assignment, and give them a day and a date when the assignment will be due.

Activity #2
    Call students to your desk (or some other private area) to discuss their papers from Writing Assignment 1. A Writing Evaluation Form is included with this unit to help structure your conferences.

    While waiting to be called for a conference, students may work on Writing Assignment 2. After students have had a writing conference with you, they should return to their seats and begin working on their writing assignment revisions while your suggestions are fresh in their minds. Be sure to give students a day and a date when their revisions are due.

# WRITING ASSIGNMENT #2 - *The Crucible*

## PROMPT

There are several interesting characters in *The Crucible*, and an understanding of the play's characters is important to an understanding of the play's themes.

Your assignment is to write a letter in which you describe one of the main characters.

Specifically, you have a choice of one of the following assignments:

1. You are Parris, writing a letter to Danforth to discredit Proctor.
2. You are Proctor, writing a letter to Danforth to explain why he should not place too much faith in Parris' opinions and accusations.
3. You are Proctor writing a letter to Danforth to discredit Abigail.
4. You are Hawthorne writing a letter to the governor describing Danforth and his handling of the Salem affair.
5. You are Parris writing a letter to Danforth about Hale's participation in the Salem affair.

## PREWRITING

One way to start is to jot down everything you know about the character who is to be described. Then jot down notes about how the writer of the letter would feel about each point you have noted about the character. Decide which points are appropriate to the purpose of your letter.

## DRAFTING

Write an introductory paragraph telling the person to whom you are writing why you are writing to him. The body of your letter should contain paragraphs giving reasons and examples. Your concluding paragraph should tell the reader of the letter what action, if any, you believe would be appropriate.

## PROMPT

When you finish the rough draft of your paper, ask a student who sits near you to read it. After reading your rough draft, he/she should tell you what he/she liked best about your work, which parts were difficult to understand, and ways in which your work could be improved. Reread your paper considering your critic's comments, and make the corrections you think are necessary.

## PROOFREADING

Do a final proofreading of your paper double-checking your grammar, spelling, organization, and the clarity of your ideas.

# WRITING EVALUATION FORM - *The Crucible*

Name _____ Date _____

Writing Assignment #1 for *The Crucible*  Grade _____

Circle One For Each Item:

Letter Format:      correct        errors noted on paper

Character Analysis:   excellent      good    fair    poor

Grammar:           correct        errors noted on paper

Spelling:           correct        errors noted on paper

Punctuation:        correct        errors noted on paper

Legibility:          excellent      good    fair    poor


Strengths:




Weaknesses:




Comments/Suggestions:

# LESSON SIXTEEN

<u>Objectives</u>

    1. To cover some important ideas presented by *The Crucible* which we haven't yet covered
    2. To focus more on interpretive, critical and personal responses than on simple facts
    3. To enhance students understanding of *The Crucible*
    4. To give students the opportunity to practice their public speaking skills

NOTE: If possible, meet with your class in your school's library. Some students may need library reference resources to help answer their questions.

<u>Activity #1</u>

    Assign one of the extra discussion questions/writing assignments to each of your students. Give them approximately fifteen minutes to formulate answers to their questions.

<u>Activity #2</u>

    Ask individual students to go to the front of the class to give the answers they have formulated for their questions. Students should field any questions other students may have regarding the topics presented in their answers. Use student responses as a springboard for discussion about the topics presented.

# EXTRA WRITING ASSIGNMENTS/DISCUSSION QUESTIONS - *The Crucible*

Interpretation

1. What actually happened on the night the girls went to the woods?

2. Where is the climax of the story? Explain your choice.

3. Are the characters in *The Crucible* stereotypes? If so, explain the usefulness of using stereotypes in the play. If they are not, explain how they merit individuality.

4. What are the conflicts in *The Crucible* and how is each resolved?

Critical

6. Compare and contrast Sarah Good and Rebecca Nurse.

7. Are the girls' actions believably motivated? Explain why or why not.

8. Explain the importance of the setting in *The Crucible*. Could this story have been set in a different time and place and still have the same effect?

9. Evaluate Arthur Miller's style of writing. How does it contribute to the value of the play?

10. What was Tituba's use as a character?

11. Compare and contrast Abigail and Mary.

12. Compare and contrast Proctor and Parris.

13. Explain how the title relates to the events of the play and the themes of *The Crucible*.

14. Explain Rebecca Nurse's role in the play. Why was she included?

15. Compare and contrast the Putnams and Proctors.

16. Discuss the theme of revenge in the play.

*The Crucible* Extra Discussion Questions page 2

Critical/Personal Response

17. Who was responsible for the deaths of the people who were wrongly convicted and hanged? Explain.

18. Pretend you have the Puritanical outlook that things are either "good" or "bad" and that there is no "inbetween" choice. Characterize each of the following characters as either "good" or "bad" and give the reasons for your choices: Abigail, Cheever, Giles Corey, Danforth, Elizabeth, Hale, Mary, Rebecca, Parris, Ann Putnam, Tituba, John Proctor.

19. What parallels can be made between the Salem witch hunt and the "witch hunt" for communists in the U.S. in the 1950's.

20. Why did most of the adults believe the children?

21. Explain how each of these people contributed to the witch hunt and its continuation: Abigail, Parris, Danforth, Mary, Betty, Ann Putnam, Hale, and Cheever.


Personal Response

22. Did you enjoy reading *The Crucible*? Why or why not?

23. The witch hunt was a form of persecution. Research to find another group of people who are being persecuted today. Write a summary of who they are and the reasons why they are being persecuted.

24. Capital punishment is a much-debated topic today. Are you for or against it? Why?


Quotations

1. Uncle, we did dance; let you tell them I confessed it--and I'll be whipped if I must be. But they're speakin' of witchcraft. Betty's not witched. (Abigail Act 1)

2. Oh, Abigail, what proper payment for my charity! Now I am undone. (Parris Act 1)

3. I never knew what pretense Salem was, I never knew the lying lessons I was taught by all these Christian women and their covenanted men! (Abigail Act 1)

4. There are wheels within wheels in this village, and fires within fires! (Mrs. Putnam Act 1)

5. I am not used to this poverty; I left a thrifty business in the Barbados to serve the Lord. (Parris Act 1)

*The Crucible* Extra Discussion Questions page 3

6. . . . while there were no witches then, there are Communists and capitalists now, and in each camp there is certain proof that spies of each side are at work undermining the other. (Miller Act 1)

7. Sex, sin, and the Devil were early linked, and so they continued to be in Salem, and are today. (Miller Act 1)

8. Parris ... *Taking some books*: My, they're heavy!
   Hale, *setting down his books*: They must be; they are weighted with authority. (Act 1)

9. She'd dare not call out such a farmer's wife but there be monstrous profit in it. She thinks to take my place, John. (Elizabeth Act 2)

10. Adultery, John. (Elizabeth Act 2)

11. There are them that will swear to anything before they'll hang; have you never thought of that? (Proctor Act 2)

12. Believe me, Mr. Nurse, if Rebecca Nurse be tainted, then nothing's left to stop the whole green world from burning. (Hale Act 2)

13. Now believe me, Proctor, how heavy be the law, all its tonnage I do carry on my back tonight. (Cheever Act 2)

14. I'll tell you what's walking Salem--vengeance is walking Salem. (Proctor Act 2)

15. Abby'll charge lechery on you, Mr. Proctor! (Mary Act 2)

16. It is a providence, and no great change; we are only what we always were, but naked now. (Proctor Act 2)

17. Beware this man, Your Excellency, this man is mischief. (Parris Act 3)

18. It were pretense, sir. (Mary Act 3)

19. That woman will never lie, Mr. Danforth. (Proctor Act 3)

20. Is every defense an attack upon the court? (Hale Act 3)

21. Do that which is good, and no harm shall come to thee. (Proctor Act 3)

*The Crucible* Extra Discussion Questions page 4

22. This man is killing his neighbors for their land! (Giles Act 3)

23. Let *you* beware, Mr. Danforth. Think you to be so mighty that the power of Hell may not turn *your* wits? Beware of it! (Abigail Act 3)

24. But it is a whore's vengeance, and you must see it; I set myself entirely in your hands. I know you must see it now. (Proctor Act 3)

25. I say--I say--God is dead! (Proctor Act 3)

26. I denounce these proceedings, I quit this court! (Hale Act 3)

27. I think, sometimes, the man has a mad look these days. (Hawthorne Act 4)

28. I think it be the cows, sir. (Cheever Act 4)

29. You cannot hang this sort. There is danger for me. I dare not step outside at night! (Parris Act 4)

30. You misunderstand, sir; I cannot pardon these when twelve are already hanged for the same crime. It is not just. (Danforth Act 4)

31. Life, woman, life is God's most precious gift; no principle, however glorious, may justify the taking of it. (Hale Act 4)

32. . . . for it may well be God damns a liar less than he that throws his life away for pride. (Hale Act 4)

33. My honesty is broke, Elizabeth; I am no good man. (Proctor Act 4)

34. God in Heaven, what is John Proctor, what is John Proctor? (Proctor Act 4)

35. I have given you my soul; leave me my name! (Proctor Act 4)

36. He have his goodness now. God forbid I take it from him! (Elizabeth Act 4)

# LESSON SEVENTEEN

Objectives
- 1. To widen the breadth of students' knowledge about the topics discussed or touched upon in *The Crucible*
- 2. To check students' nonfiction reading assignments

Activity

Ask each student to give a brief oral report about the nonfiction work he/she read for the nonfiction reading assignment. Your criteria for evaluating this report will vary depending on the level of your students. You may wish for students to give a complete report without using notes of any kind, or you may want students to read directly from a written report, or you may want to do something in between these two extremes. Just make students aware of your criteria in ample time for them to prepare their reports.

Start with one student's report. After that, ask if anyone else in the class has read on a topic related to the first student's report. If no one has, choose another student at random. After each report, be sure to ask if anyone has a report related to the one just completed. That will help keep a continuity during the discussion of the reports.


# LESSON EIGHTEEN

Objective

To review the main ideas presented in *The Crucible*

Activity #1

Choose one of the review games/activities and spend your class period as outlined there. Some materials for these activities are located Unit Resource section of this unit.

Activity #2

Remind students that the Unit Test will be in the next class meeting. Stress the review of the Study Guides and their class notes as a last minute, brush-up review for homework.

## REVIEW GAMES/ACTIVITIES - *The Crucible*

1. Ask the class to make up a unit test for *The Crucible*. The test should have 4 sections: matching, true/false, short answer, and essay. Students may use 1/2 period to make the test and then swap papers and use the other 1/2 class period to take a test a classmate has devised. (open book). You may want to use the unit test included in this packet or take questions from the students' unit tests to formulate your own test.

2. Take 1/2 period for students to make up true and false questions (including the answers). Collect the papers and divide the class into two teams. Draw a big tic-tac-toe board on the chalk board. Make one team X and one team O. Ask questions to each side, giving each student one turn. If the question is answered correctly, that students' team's letter (X or O) is placed in the box. If the answer is incorrect, no mark is placed in the box. The object is to get three marks in a row like tic-tac-toe. You may want to keep track of the number of games won for each team.

3. Take 1/2 period for students to make up questions (true/false and short answer). Collect the questions. Divide the class into two teams. You'll alternate asking questions to individual members of teams A & B (like in a spelling bee). The question keeps going from A to B until it is correctly answered, then a new question is asked. A correct answer does not allow the team to get another question. Correct answers are +2 points; incorrect answers are -1 point.

4. Have students pair up and quiz each other from their study guides and class notes.

5. Give students a *The Crucible* crossword puzzle to complete.

6. Divide your class into two teams. Use the *Crucible* crossword words with their letters jumbled as a word list. Student 1 from Team A faces off against Student 1 from Team B. You write the first jumbled word on the board. The first student (1A or 1B) to unscramble the word wins the chance for his/her team to score points. If 1A wins the jumble, go to student 2A and give him/her a clue. He/she must give you the correct word which matches that clue. If he/she does, Team A scores a point, and you give student 3A a clue for which you expect another correct response. Continue giving Team A clues until some team member makes an incorrect response. An incorrect response sends the game back to the jumbled-word face off, this time with students 2A and 2B. Instead of repeating giving clues to the first few students of each team, continue with the student after the one who gave the last incorrect response on the team. For example, if Team B wins the jumbled-word face-off, and student 5B gave the last incorrect answer for Team B, you would start this round of clue questions with student 6B, and so on. The team with the most points wins!

# UNIT TESTS

# WRITING ASSIGNMENT #3 - *The Crucible*

## PROMPT
You have read the play *The Crucible*, have had discussions about the ideas and characters presented in the play, and have become educated about a variety of topics related to it.

Now, thinking about all you have learned, tell who, in your opinion, is to blame for the deaths of those innocent Puritans who died during the witch hunt. Be specific and use examples from the text to support your ideas.

## PREWRITING
One way to start is to list all the possible candidates who could be held responsible. Next to each, jot down all the reasons they could be blamed. Then, looking at that information, decide which bears the ultimate responsibility.

## DRAFTING
Your introductory paragraph could contain information about those who bear some responsibility for the deaths followed by something like, ". . . but the ultimate responsibility for the deaths of the innocent Puritans is borne by _____."

Following the introductory paragraph, the paragraphs in the body of your paper should each give a reason why you think that person is responsible. Within each of the body paragraphs, you should support your statements with as many facts and examples from the text as possible.

Your final paragraph should give your final thoughts and conclusions.

## PROMPT
When you finish the rough draft of your paper, ask a student who sits near you to read it. After reading your rough draft, he/she should tell you what he/she liked best about your work, which parts were difficult to understand, and ways in which your work could be improved. Reread your paper considering your critic's comments, and make the corrections you think are necessary.

## PROOFREADING
Do a final proofreading of your paper double-checking your grammar, spelling, organization, and the clarity of your ideas.

# SHORT ANSWER UNIT TEST #1 - *The Crucible*

I. Matching/Identify

___ 1. Abigail          A. He arrested Elizabeth

___ 2. Betty            B. Thomas or Ann; Their babies died

___ 3. Cheever          C. Judge

___ 4. Corey            D. Mrs. Nurse; maintained her innocence

___ 5. Danforth         E. Expert spirit remover

___ 6. Elizabeth        F. John; had an affair with Abigail

___ 7. Hale             G. Parris' daughter

___ 8. Miller           H. Parris' slave from Barbados

___ 9. Mary             I. John's wife

___ 10. Rebecca         J. She was the primary cause of the witch trials

___ 11. Parris          K. He didn't like Proctor & Proctor didn't like him

___ 12. Putnam          L. Gave a poppet to Elizabeth

___ 13. Tituba          M. He was pressed to death

___ 14. Proctor         N. Author

*Crucible* Short Answer Unit Test 1 Page 2

II. Short Answer

1. Explain how the witch-hunt years were a time of "general revenge."

2. Explain the political relationship between the Putnam and Nurse families.

3. What is Proctor's reason for his not regularly attending church?

4. Why doesn't Proctor want Mary to go back to court?

5. Why does Elizabeth think Abigail wants to kill her?

6. Explain the significance of the needle in the "poppet."

7. What is Parris' argument against Proctor?

8. Of what does Giles accuse Putnam?

*Crucible* Short Answer Unit Test 1 Page 3

9. What is Hale's problem as Proctor and his friends present evidence to Danforth?

10. Explain Danforth's reason that a pardon would not be just.

11. What "confession" did Elizabeth make to John?

12. What did Proctor do after he signed the confession? Why?

*Crucible* Short Answer Unit Test 1 Page 4

III. Composition

Paragraphs: Write a one-paragraph answer for each of the following:

1. Explain how the play shows the individual against authority.

2. Explain how Puritanism was a motivating force in the witch hunt.

*Crucible* Short Answer Unit Test 1 Page 5

IV. Vocabulary

    Listen to the vocabulary word and spell it.
    After you have spelled all the words, go back and write down the definitions.

1.

2.

3.

4.

5.

6.

7.

8.

9.

10.

# SHORT ANSWER UNIT TEST 2 - *The Crucible*

I. Matching/Identify

___ 1. Abigail      A. Judge

___ 2. Betty      B. John's wife

___ 3. Cheever      C. He didn't like Proctor & Proctor didn't like him

___ 4. Corey      D. Gave a poppet to Elizabeth

___ 5. Danforth      E. Author

___ 6. Elizabeth      F. She was the primary cause of the witch trials

___ 7. Hale      G. Parris' daughter

___ 8. Miller      H. Parris' slave from Barbados

___ 9. Mary      I. Thomas or Ann; Their babies died

___ 10. Rebecca      J. John; had an affair with Abigail

___ 11. Parris      K. He arrested Elizabeth

___ 12. Putnam      L. Mrs. Nurse; maintained her innocence

___ 13. Tituba      M. He was pressed to death

___ 14. Proctor      N. Expert spirit remover

*Crucible* Short Answer Unit Test 2 Page 2

II. Short Answer

1. Why is Thomas Putnam bitter?

2. What happened between Abigail and John Proctor prior to the opening of the play?

3. What is Rebecca's explanation of the girls' behavior?

4. What is Proctor's reason for his not regularly attending church?

5. Where does Elizabeth want John to go at the beginning of Act Two, and what does she want him to do there?

6. Why did Hale come to Proctor's house?

7. What things are "suspicious" about Proctor and his family?

8. Explain the significance of the needle in the "poppet."

9. Why doesn't Mary want to testify about the doll?

*Crucible* Short Answer Unit Test 2 Page 3

10. Of what does Giles accuse Putnam?

11. What happens to Proctor?

12. What did Abigail do?

13. Explain Danforth's reason that a pardon would not be just.

14. What did Proctor do after he signed the confession? Why?

*Crucible* Short Answer Unit Test 2 Page 4

III. Composition
   Write a one-paragraph answer for each of these:

1. What is the effect of confession in the play? Give examples.

2. How was Puritanism a motivating force in the witch hunt?

*Crucible* Short Answer Unit Test 2 Page 5

IV. Vocabulary
    Listen to the vocabulary words.
    Write them down, then go back and write down definitions for them.

1.

2.

3.

4.

5.

6.

7.

8.

9.

10.

# KEY: SHORT ANSWER UNIT TESTS - *The Crucible*

The short answer questions are taken directly from the study guides.
If you need to look up the answers, you will find them in the study guide section.

Answers to the composition questions will vary depending on your
class discussions and the level of your students.

For the vocabulary section of the test, choose ten of the words from the
vocabulary lists to read orally for your students.

The answers to the matching section of the test are below.

Answers to the matching section of the Advanced Short Answer Unit Test
are the same as for Short Answer Unit Test #2.

| **Test #1** | **Test #2** |
|---|---|
| 1. J | 1. F |
| 2. G | 2. G |
| 3. A | 3. K |
| 4. M | 4. M |
| 5. C | 5. A |
| 6. I | 6. B |
| 7. E | 7. N |
| 8. N | 8. E |
| 9. L | 9. D |
| 10. D | 10. L |
| 11. K | 11. C |
| 12. B | 12. I |
| 13. H | 13. H |
| 14. F | 14. J |

# ADVANCED SHORT ANSWER UNIT TEST - *The Crucible*

I. Matching/Identify

___ 1. Abigail           A. Judge

___ 2. Betty             B. John's wife

___ 3. Cheever         C. He didn't like Proctor & Proctor didn't like him

___ 4. Corey            D. Gave a poppet to Elizabeth

___ 5. Danforth        E. Author

___ 6. Elizabeth       F. She was the primary cause of the witch trials

___ 7. Hale             G. Parris' daughter

___ 8. Miller           H. Parris' slave from Barbados

___ 9. Mary            I. Thomas or Ann; Their babies died

___ 10. Rebecca        J. John; had an affair with Abigail

___ 11. Parris           K. He arrested Elizabeth

___ 12. Putnam         L. Mrs. Nurse; maintained her innocence

___ 13. Tituba          M. He was pressed to death

___ 14. Proctor         N. Expert spirit remover

*Crucible* Advanced Short Answer Unit Test Page 2

II. Short Answer
1. Compare and contrast Sarah Good and Rebecca

2. Explain the importance of the setting in *The Crucible*. Could this story have been set in a different time and place and still have the same effect?

3. Compare and contrast Proctor and Parris.

4. Discuss the theme of revenge in the play.

2. Where is the climax of the story? Explain your choice.

*Crucible* Advanced Short Answer Unit Test Page 3

III. Quotations
    Explain the importance, meaning and/or significance of each of the following quotations.

1. Oh, Abigail, what proper payment for my charity! Now I am undone. (Parris Act 1)

2. There are wheels within wheels in this village, and fires within fires! (Mrs. Putnam Act 1)

3. Do that which is good, and no harm shall come to thee. (Proctor Act 3)

4. You cannot hang this sort. There is danger for me. I dare not step outside at night! (Parris Act 4)

5. You misunderstand, sir; I cannot pardon these when twelve are already hanged for the same crime. It is not just. (Danforth Act 4)

6. . . . . for it may well be God damns a liar less than he that throws his life away for pride. (Hale Act 4)

7. I have given you my soul; leave me my name! (Proctor Act 4)

8. He have his goodness now. God forbid I take it from him! (Elizabeth Act 4)

*Crucible* Advanced Short Answer Unit Test Page 4

IV. Vocabulary

Listen to the words and write them down. After you have written them all down, write a paragraph in which you use all of the words. The paragraph must relate in some way to *The Crucible*.

# MULTIPLE CHOICE UNIT TEST 1 - *The Crucible*

I. Matching/Identify

    1. Abigail               A. John's wife
    2. Betty                 B. Expert spirit remover
    3. Cheever            C. Parris' daughter
    4. Corey               D. He didn't like Proctor & Proctor didn't like him
    5. Danforth          E. She was the primary cause of the witch trials
    6. Elizabeth         F. Parris' slave from Barbados
    7. Hale                 G. Judge
    8. Miller               H. John; had an affair with Abigail
    9. Mary                I. Author
   10. Rebecca           J. Thomas or Ann; Their babies died
   11. Parris              K. Mrs. Nurse; maintained her innocence
   12. Putnam            L. He was pressed to death
   13. Tituba              M. Gave a poppet to Elizabeth
   14. Proctor             N. He arrested Elizabeth

II. True or False?

1. The Puritans came to this country for religious freedom; however, when they got here they persecuted others as they had been persecuted. They turned their colony into a place almost as bad as the place they had left.

2. Being under such strict laws and commandments, the Puritans had to repress a lot of their anger and spirit of revenge towards their neighbors. When the witch hunts started, it was an excellent opportunity for them to "let their hair down" and get revenge on their neighbors for whatever petty squabbles they had been having.

3. Thomas Putnam was a kind and gentle man of good character.

4. Parris was in charge of a congregation that was split; his ministry was not popular with everyone.

5. The Nurses were not liked by the Putnams because of some land disputes, and this conflict was somewhat revenged by the Putnams when Ann Putnam accused Rebecca of bewitching her newborn babies (implying she was responsible for their deaths).

6. Proctor doesn't attend church because he doesn't like Parris.

7. Rev. John Hale has come to Salem to take Parris's place.

*Crucible* Multiple Choice Unit Test 1 Page 2

III. Multiple Choice

1. Why does Elizabeth think Abigail wants to kill her?
    a. She is sick and a little paranoid.
    b. She believes that Abby wants to take her place as John's wife.
    c. She believes Abby is bewitched and will try to destroy anything good.
    d. a & c

2. Why did Hale come to Proctor's house?
    a. He wanted to find out why Parris was so bitter.
    b. He wanted to question them prior to seeing them in court.
    c. He wanted to find out if the rumor about John and Abby was true.
    d. All of the above

3. What things are "suspicious" about Proctor and his family?
    a. Proctor does not go to church regularly.
    b. The youngest son has not been baptized.
    c. He could not remember all of the commandments.
    d. All of the above

4. On what charge(s) was Rebecca Nurse arrested?
    a. The murder of Goody Putnam's babies
    b. Impious conduct
    c. Conduct unbefitting a Puritan woman
    d. Inability to say the ten commandments from memory

5. What is the deciding factor in Elizabeth's arrest?
    a. Her inability to recite the ten commandments
    b. Her possession of the doll with a needle in it
    c. The fact that she has not had her son baptized
    d. Abby's testimony

6. What is Parris' argument against Proctor?
    a. Parris says that Proctor is trying to overthrow the court.
    b. Parris says that Proctor is biased because of his position between Abigail and Elizabeth.
    c. Parris says that Proctor is just getting even with him.
    d. b & c

*Crucible* Multiple Choice Unit Test 1 Page 3

7. What does Mary tell Danforth?
    a. Abigail is not evil; she's just in love with Proctor.
    b. The girls have been lying.
    c. Tituba was responsible for their actions in the woods.
    d. Abigail gave Elizabeth the doll.

8. Of what does Giles accuse Putnam?
    a. He accuses him of killing his neighbors for their land.
    b. He accuses him of being in service to the devil.
    c. He accuses him of taking advantage of the girls.
    d. He accuses him of being a hypocrite.

9. What is Hale's problem as Proctor and his friends present evidence to Danforth?
    a. He worries about his own safety from the girls' accusations.
    b. He sees that he has been a failure at removing witchcraft from Salem.
    c. He thinks his reputation will be hurt.
    d. He begins to realize that the people who had been accused and sentenced so far could very well have been innocent.

10. What happens to Proctor?
    a. He is jailed for being a lecher.
    b. He is jailed for lying to the court.
    c. He is jailed for adultery.
    d. He is jailed for his contempt of the court and his suspicious activities.

11. What did Abigail do?
    a. Abigail stole money from Parris and disappeared.
    b. Abigail killed herself.
    c. Abigail begged for everyone's forgiveness.
    d. Abigail confessed that she and the others had been lying.

12. Why has Hale come back to Salem?
    a. To free the unjustly jailed.
    b. To encourage the accused to confess and save their lives
    c. To discredit the girls
    d. All of the above

13. What did Proctor do after he signed the confession?
    a. He collapsed, a broken man.
    b. He tore it up.
    c. He begged Elizabeth to forgive him.
    d. a & c

*Crucible* Multiple Choice Unit Test 1 Page 4

IV. Vocabulary

1. base            A. False statement maliciously or knowingly made

2. bemused      B. Summoned by oath or spell

3. beguile        C. Postponement of punishment

4. penitence     D. Work of divine direction

5. avidly         E. Enthusiastically

6. reprieve       F. Disaster

7. tainted        G. Laws, decrees or edicts

8. pallor         H. Delude; cheat; divert

9. blasphemy     I. Extreme paleness

10. effrontery     J. Militant supporter of a party, cause faction, or idea

11. contentious    K. Awkward

12. evade         L. Having low moral standards; contemptible; inferior

13. statutes       M. An irreverent or impious act or utterance

14. providence    N. Quarrelsome

15. calumny      O. Having a moral defect; infected

16. daft           P. Performing of penance

17. ineptly        Q. Escape or avoid by cleverness or deceit

18. conjured      R. Confused

19. calamity      S. Audacity; insulting boldness

20. partisan      T. Crazy; foolish; stupid

MULTIPLE CHOICE UNIT TEST 1 ANSWER SHEET - *The Crucible*

| I. Matching | II. True or False | III. Multiple Choice | IV. Vocabulary |
|---|---|---|---|
| 1. ___ | 1. ___ | 1. ___ | 1. ___ |
| 2. ___ | 2. ___ | 2. ___ | 2. ___ |
| 3. ___ | 3. ___ | 3. ___ | 3. ___ |
| 4. ___ | 4. ___ | 4. ___ | 4. ___ |
| 5. ___ | 5. ___ | 5. ___ | 5. ___ |
| 6. ___ | 6. ___ | 6. ___ | 6. ___ |
| 7. ___ | 7. ___ | 7. ___ | 7. ___ |
| 8. ___ |  | 8. ___ | 8. ___ |
| 9. ___ |  | 9. ___ | 9. ___ |
| 10. ___ |  | 10. ___ | 10. ___ |
| 11. ___ |  | 11. ___ | 11. ___ |
| 12. ___ |  | 12. ___ | 12. ___ |
| 13. ___ |  | 13. ___ | 13. ___ |
| 14. ___ |  |  | 14. ___ |
|  |  |  | 15. ___ |
|  |  |  | 16. ___ |
|  |  |  | 17. ___ |
|  |  |  | 18. ___ |
|  |  |  | 19. ___ |
|  |  |  | 20. ___ |

# ANSWER KEY: MULTIPLE CHOICE UNIT TEST 1 - *The Crucible*

| I. Matching | II. True or False | III. Multiple Choice | IV. Vocabulary |
|---|---|---|---|
| 1. E | 1. T | 1. B | 1. L |
| 2. C | 2. T | 2. B | 2. R |
| 3. N | 3. F | 3. D | 3. H |
| 4. L | 4. T | 4. A | 4. P |
| 5. G | 5. T | 5. B | 5. E |
| 6. A | 6. T | 6. A | 6. C |
| 7. B | 7. F | 7. B | 7. O |
| 8. I | | 8. A | 8. I |
| 9. M | | 9. D | 9. M |
| 10. K | | 10. D | 10. S |
| 11. D | | 11. A | 11. N |
| 12. J | | 12. B | 12. Q |
| 13. F | | 13. B | 13. G |
| 14. H | | | 14. D |
| | | | 15. A |
| | | | 16. T |
| | | | 17. K |
| | | | 18. B |
| | | | 19. F |
| | | | 20. J |

# MULTIPLE CHOICE UNIT TEST 2 - *The Crucible*

I. Matching/Identify

    1. Abigail      A. He didn't like Proctor & Proctor didn't like him

    2. Betty      B. John's wife

    3. Cheever      C. Mrs. Nurse; maintained her innocence

    4. Corey      D. Judge

    5. Danforth      E. He was pressed to death

    6. Elizabeth      F. He arrested Elizabeth

    7. Hale      G. Parris' slave from Barbados

    8. Miller      H. Parris' daughter

    9. Mary      I. She was the primary cause of the witch trials

    10. Rebecca      J. John; had an affair with Abigail

    11. Parris      K. Thomas or Ann; Their babies died

    12. Putnam      L. Author

    13. Tituba      M. Expert spirit remover

    14. Proctor      N. Gave a poppet to Elizabeth

*Crucible* Multiple Choice Unit Test 2 Page 2

II. Multiple Choice: Identify the speaker

**A**= Abigail  **B**=Parris  **C**=Proctor  **D**=Elizabeth  **E**=Mary  **F**=John  **G**=Hale  **H**=Cheever

1. Uncle, we did dance; let you tell them I confessed it--and I'll be whipped if I must be. But they're speakin' of witchcraft. Betty's not witched.

2. I am not used to this poverty; I left a thrifty business in the Barbados to serve the Lord.

3. She thinks to take my place, John.

4. There are them that will swear to anything before they'll hang; have you never thought of that?

5. ... if Rebecca Nurse be tainted, then nothing's left to stop the whole green world from burning.

6. . . . how heavy be the law, all its tonnage I do carry on my back tonight.

7. Abby'll charge lechery on you, Mr. Proctor!

8. It were pretense, sir.

9. Do that which is good, and no harm shall come to thee.

10. I denounce these proceedings, and I quit this court.

11. You cannot hang this sort. There is danger for me.

12. I have given you my soul; leave me my name!

*Crucible* Multiple Choice Unit Test 2 Page 3
III. Multiple Choice
1. What gift did Mary give Elizabeth?
	a. A Bible
	b. A doll
	c. A basket of flowers
	d. a & c

2. Why does Elizabeth think Abigail wants to kill her?
	a. She is sick and a little paranoid.
	b. She believes that Abby wants to take her place as John's wife.
	c. She believes Abby is bewitched and will try to destroy anything good.
	d. a & d

3. Hale asks Elizabeth if she believes in witches. What is her reply?
	a. If she is accused of being a witch, she cannot believe in witches.
	b. If the Bible says that witches exist, she cannot dispute the Bible.
	c. She does not believe the girls are telling the truth.
	d. a & b

4. On what charge(s) was Rebecca Nurse arrested?
	a. The murder of Goody Putnam's babies
	b. Impious conduct
	c. Conduct unbefitting a Puritan woman
	d. Inability to say the ten commandments from memory

5. What is the deciding factor in Elizabeth's arrest?
	a. Her inability to recite the ten commandments
	b. Her possession of the doll with a needle in it
	c. The fact that she has not had her son baptized
	d. Abby's testimony

6. Why do Giles and Francis want to see Danforth?
	a. They intend to beat him to his senses.
	b. They want to explain their roles in the witchcraft scheme.
	c. They want to persuade the judge that their wives are good women.
	d. They want to explain how Parris is at fault.

7. What is Parris' argument against Proctor?
	a. Parris says that Proctor is trying to overthrow the court.
	b. Parris says that Proctor is biased because of his position between Abigail and Elizabeth.
	c. Parris says that Proctor is just getting even with him.
	d. b & c

*Crucible* Multiple Choice Unit Test 2 Page 4

8. What does Mary tell Danforth?
    a. Abigail is not evil; she's just in love with Proctor.
    b. The girls have been lying.
    c. Tituba was responsible for their actions in the woods.
    d. Abigail gave Elizabeth the doll.

9. Why did Danforth grant Elizabeth extra time?
    a. He didn't blame her for being jealous of Abigail.
    b. She was trying to convince John to confess.
    c. She said she was pregnant.
    d. He almost believed Mary's story.

10. What is Hale's problem as Proctor and his friends present evidence to Danforth?
    a. He worries about his own safety from the girls' accusations.
    b. He sees that he has been a failure at removing witchcraft from Salem.
    c. He thinks his reputation will be hurt.
    d. He begins to realize that the people who had been accused and sentenced so far could very well have been innocent.

11. What happens to Proctor?
    a. He is jailed for being a lecher.
    b. He is jailed for lying to the court.
    c. He is jailed for adultery.
    d. He is jailed for his contempt of the court and his suspicious activities.

12. Explain Danforth's reason that a pardon would not be a good idea.
    a. If he would pardon the remaining accused, the people who had been hanged would have died in vain.
    b. Rather than admit that the court could have been wrong and therefore admit the others may have been hanged unjustly, he thought it better to continue hanging people so all accused would get the same treatment from the court.
    c. The citizens would lose respect for the court and anarchy would prevail.
    d. a & b

13. Why has Hale come back to Salem?
    a. To free the unjustly jailed.
    b. To encourage the accused to confess and save their lives
    c. To discredit the girls
    d. All of the above

*Crucible* Multiple Choice Unit Test 2 Page 5

IV. Vocabulary

1. indictment
2. faction
3. ascertain
4. lechery
5. reprieve
6. adamant
7. province
8. inert
9. ineptly
10. calumny
11. penitence
12. fraud
13. menacingly
14. licentious
15. manifest
16. sarcastical
17. bemused
18. audible
19. diabolism
20. conjured

A. Awkward
B. False statement maliciously or knowingly made
C. Expressing mocking or contemptuous remarks
D. Postponement of punishment
E. Having no regard for accepted rules or standards
F. Performing of penance
G. Able to be heard
H. Deliberate deception for unfair or unlawful gain
I. Unable to move or act
J. Small group of people, usually contentious, within a larger group
K. Witchcraft; sorcery
L. Promiscuity
M. Confused
N. Summoned by oath or spell
O. Statement of criminal charges
P. Something apparent to the sight or understanding
Q. Work of divine direction
R. Firm in purpose or opinion; unyielding
S. Find out
T. Threateningly

# ANSWER SHEET MULTIPLE CHOICE UNIT TEST 2 - *The Crucible*

| I. Matching | II. True or False | III. Multiple Choice | IV. Vocabulary |
|---|---|---|---|
| 1. ___ | 1. ___ | 1. ___ | 1. ___ |
| 2. ___ | 2. ___ | 2. ___ | 2. ___ |
| 3. ___ | 3. ___ | 3. ___ | 3. ___ |
| 4. ___ | 4. ___ | 4. ___ | 4. ___ |
| 5. ___ | 5. ___ | 5. ___ | 5. ___ |
| 6. ___ | 6. ___ | 6. ___ | 6. ___ |
| 7. ___ | 7. ___ | 7. ___ | 7. ___ |
| 8. ___ | 8. ___ | 8. ___ | 8. ___ |
| 9. ___ | 9. ___ | 9. ___ | 9. ___ |
| 10. ___ | 10. ___ | 10. ___ | 10. ___ |
| 11. ___ | 11. ___ | 11. ___ | 11. ___ |
| 12. ___ | 12. ___ | 12. ___ | 12. ___ |
| 13. ___ | | 13. ___ | 13. ___ |
| 14. ___ | | | 14. ___ |
| | | | 15. ___ |
| | | | 16. ___ |
| | | | 17. ___ |
| | | | 18. ___ |
| | | | 19. ___ |
| | | | 20. ___ |

# ANSWER KEY: MULTIPLE CHOICE UNIT TEST 2 - *The Crucible*

| I. Matching | II. Identify | III. Multiple Choice | IV. Vocabulary |
|---|---|---|---|
| 1. I | 1. A | 1. B | 1. O |
| 2. H | 2. B | 2. B | 2. J |
| 3. F | 3. D | 3. D | 3. S |
| 4. E | 4. F | 4. A | 4. L |
| 5. D | 5. G | 5. B | 5. D |
| 6. B | 6. H | 6. C | 6. R |
| 7. M | 7. E | 7. A | 7. Q |
| 8. L | 8. E | 8. B | 8. I |
| 9. N | 9. F | 9. C | 9. A |
| 10. C | 10. G | 10. D | 10. B |
| 11. A | 11. B | 11. D | 11. F |
| 12. K | 12. F | 12. D | 12. H |
| 13. G | | 13. B | 13. T |
| 14. J | | | 14. E |
| | | | 15. P |
| | | | 16. C |
| | | | 17. M |
| | | | 18. G |
| | | | 19. K |
| | | | 20. N |

# UNIT RESOURCE MATERIALS

## BULLETIN BOARD IDEAS - *The Crucible*

1. Save one corner of the board for the best of students' *Crucible* writing assignments.

2. Do the bulletin board suggested in Lesson One as an introductory activity (posting articles about Puritanism and witchcraft).

3. Make a bulletin board on which you pin, in a random order, all the reasons given for why the witch hunt took place. When the students finish reading the play, have them put the reasons in order from the most important reason to the least important reason.

4. Take one of the word search puzzles from the extra activities packet and with a marker copy it over in a large size on the bulletin board. Write the clue words to find to one side. Invite students prior to and after class to find the words and circle them on the bulletin board.

5. Do a bulletin board about careers in law, law enforcement, the justice system, and religion.

6. Post a map of the United States with a big red star to show where Salem is.

7. Post articles about famous trials that have taken place (or trials that are currently taking place).

8. Make a historical time line showing what else was going on in history in the same era as the witch trials.

9. Write several of the most significant quotations from the play onto the board on brightly colored paper.

10. Make a bulletin board listing the vocabulary words for this unit. As you complete sections of the play and discuss the vocabulary for each section, write the definitions on the bulletin board. (If your board is one students face frequently, it will help them learn the words.)

# EXTRA ACTIVITIES

One of the difficulties in teaching literature is that all students don't read at the same speed. One student who likes to read may take the play home and finish it in a day or two. Sometimes a few students finish the in-class assignments early. The problem, then, is finding suitable extra activities for students.

The best thing I've found is to keep a little library in the classroom. For this unit on *The Crucible*, you might check out from the school library other related books and articles about how our justice system works, careers in the justice system or religion, theocracy, Puritans, witchcraft, unexplained phenomena, famous lies throughout history, American history from 1600-1650, or revenge in history. Other plays by Arthur Miller or critical reviews of *The Crucible* might also be of interest to students.

Other things you may keep on hand are puzzles. We have made some relating directly to *The Crucible* for you. Feel free to duplicate them.

Some students may like to draw. You might devise a contest or allow some extra-credit grade for students who draw characters or scenes from *The Crucible*. Note, too, that if the students do not want to keep their drawings you may pick up some extra bulletin board materials this way. If you have a contest and you supply the prize (a CD or something like that perhaps), you could, possibly, make the drawing itself a non-refundable entry fee.

The pages which follow contain games, puzzles and worksheets. The keys, when appropriate, immediately follow the puzzle or worksheet. There are two main groups of activities: one group for the unit; that is, generally relating to the *Crucible* text, and another group of activities related strictly to the *Crucible* vocabulary.

Directions for these games, puzzles and worksheets are self-explanatory. The object here is to provide you with extra materials you may use in any way you choose.

# MORE ACTIVITIES - *The Crucible*

1. Make a complete production of *The Crucible* and perform it for other classes in your school.

2. Have students make a model of Salem, including all the important places mentioned in the play. You could have them either stick only to the details given in the play -- or you could let them create the details which are not given.

3. Show the film *The Crucible* after you have completed reading the play in class. Have students evaluate the movie and compare/contrast it with the written play.

4. Have students design a playbill for *The Crucible*

5. Have students design a bulletin board (ready to be put up; not just sketched) for *The Crucible*.

6. Take a field trip to see how our justice system works. Go to your local courthouse and sit in on a criminal jury trial. (This might be good in preparation for writing the scene for Abby's trial.)

7. Discuss recent horror films which portray elements of witchcraft.

8. Make a lesson around "lies." Discuss the different kinds of lies people tell -- and why people tell lies. Perhaps have some of your students tell times they have lied and gotten into trouble. Give some examples of times when people have been caught lying. (A look back at politicians in the last 20 years should give you some great, classic examples.)

9. Make a lesson around "forgiveness." Discuss hypothetical situations like: "If you Elizabeth, would you forgive John?" "If you were John would you forgive Abby?" "If you were Giles, would you forgive the men who added the weights?" and so on. Talk about the importance of forgiveness, what it means to "forgive" someone, and if there are times when "forgiveness" is impossible. Cite times in history or in fiction when forgiveness has played an important role.

10. Have an attorney come to your classroom to discuss the judicial system, a specific trial, the duties of a lawyer, or just general questions students might have about what is and is not legal. If you could get the lawyer to agree to it, a discussion of the Salem witch trials might be interesting from a lawyer's point of view.

# WORD SEARCH - *The Crucible*

```
F  B  C  H  E  E  V  E  R  S  O  U  L  G  G  M  H  D  L  E
I  J  B  S  A  I  T  I  T  U  B  A  M  Z  T  A  B  A  H  S
R  K  J  P  E  N  R  O  H  T  W  A  H  C  O  R  E  Y  L  N
E  Y  P  F  G  D  G  P  P  M  N  C  H  C  W  Y  I  I  L  E
W  A  V  I  V  I  G  O  L  T  T  C  L  V  O  M  V  A  J  T
O  L  S  S  Q  V  S  P  U  I  C  E  P  Y  R  E  N  S  L  E
O  P  A  R  R  I  S  P  W  B  T  B  R  V  S  D  E  D  T  R
D  H  B  D  E  D  D  E  I  S  X  E  W  R  H  L  O  C  S  P
F  C  I  D  T  U  K  T  E  R  T  R  U  F  I  G  A  W  E  S
R  R  G  G  T  A  W  N  F  L  I  N  J  G  P  D  P  G  R  C
J  U  A  Q  I  L  O  F  U  D  G  T  B  A  B  I  E  S  O  E
V  H  I  N  B  H  H  D  B  A  O  S  S  O  I  P  G  V  F  N
W  C  L  C  C  Z  A  D  M  N  O  H  O  X  B  J  D  Z  I  E
E  C  N  E  D  I  V  E  N  C  D  K  P  V  L  X  U  C  P  L
B  E  T  T  Y  H  S  N  X  E  S  K  P  M  E  H  J  K  P  F
```

Alone; not as a member of a group (10)
Ann or Thomas (6)
Bad (4)
Betty's father and Abigail's uncle (6)
Decision maker in court (5)
Division of an act (5)
Examination of evidence to determine guilt or innocence (5)
Ghosts, beings (7)
Gift from Mary to Elizabeth (6)
Giles (5)
God's house (6)
He arrests Elizabeth (7)
He thinks of a test for Mary (9)
He was an expert spirit remover (4)
If Proctor tells the truth, he will save his (4)
Many of Mrs. Putnam's have died (6)
Material proof (8)
Meeting place of Tituba and the devil (6)
Method of execution using a rope (4)
Move with rhythm (5)
Mr. Corey (5)
Mr. Nurse (7)

Mrs. Nurse (7)
Object of the Putnams' dispute with the Nurses (4)
One who tells the truth is this (6)
Opposite of bad (4)
Parris wanted a deed and this along with his salary (8)
Parris' daughter (5)
Parris' slave woman from Barbados (6)
Play division (3)
Reading material (5)
Rebecca (5)
Satan (5)
She is the primary cause of the witch hunts (7)
She wants Abby to tell the truth (4)
Something that shows the existence of a fact (4)
Story written to be performed on the stage (4)
The Christian holy book (5)
The Creator (3)
The act of pretending (8)
The commandment Proctor forgets (8)
Thomas Putnam was this about his situation in life (6)
To adore (7)
Woman who practices witchcraft (5)

The numbers following the clues are the number of letters in the answer.

# WORD SEARCH ANSWER KEY - *The Crucible*

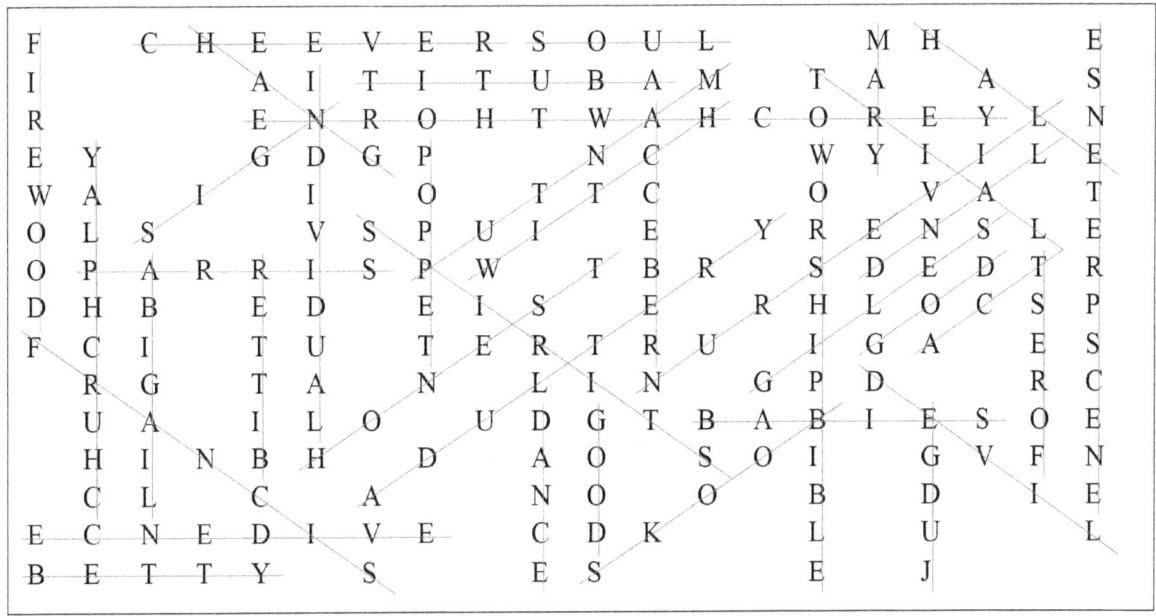

Alone; not as a member of a group (10)
Ann or Thomas (6)
Bad (4)
Betty's father and Abigail's uncle (6)
Decision maker in court (5)
Division of an act (5)
Examination of evidence to determine guilt or innocence (5)
Ghosts, beings (7)
Gift from Mary to Elizabeth (6)
Giles (5)
God's house (6)
He arrests Elizabeth (7)
He thinks of a test for Mary (9)
He was an expert spirit remover (4)
If Proctor tells the truth, he will save his (4)
Many of Mrs. Putnam's have died (6)
Material proof (8)
Meeting place of Tituba and the devil (6)
Method of execution using a rope (4)
Move with rhythm (5)
Mr. Corey (5)
Mr. Nurse (7)

Mrs. Nurse (7)
Object of the Putnams' dispute with the Nurses (4)
One who tells the truth is this (6)
Opposite of bad (4)
Parris wanted a deed and this along with his salary (8)
Parris' daughter (5)
Parris' slave woman from Barbados (6)
Play division (3)
Reading material (5)
Rebecca (5)
Satan (5)
She is the primary cause of the witch hunts (7)
She wants Abby to tell the truth (4)
Something that shows the existence of a fact (4)
Story written to be performed on the stage (4)
The Christian holy book (5)
The Creator (3)
The act of pretending (8)
The commandment Proctor forgets (8)
Thomas Putnam was this about his situation in life (6)
To adore (7)
Woman who practices witchcraft (5)

# CROSSWORD - *The Crucible*

# CROSSWORD CLUES - *The Crucible*

## ACROSS

1. Gift from Mary to Elizabeth
3. Thomas Putnam was this about his situation in life
9. Parris' slave woman from Barbados
10. Parris wanted salary, deed & this
11. Giles
12. Parris' daughter
14. Object of the Putnams' dispute with the Nurses
15. He was an expert spirit remover
19. Mrs. Nurse
21. She is the primary cause of the witch hunts
22. Division of an act
24. Nagging conscience
25. Method of execution using a rope
28. Move with rhythm
30. If proctor tells the truth, he will save this
31. Something that shows the existence of a fact
32. One who tells the truth is this
33. Meeting place of Tituba and the devil
34. Decision maker in court
36. Mr. Nurse
37. John; he tries to make people see the truth
38. God's house

## DOWN

1. Betty's father & Abigail's uncle
2. Ann or Thomas
3. The Christian Holy Book
4. Bad
5. Reading material
6. She wants Abby to tell the truth
7. Satan
8. The commandment Proctor forgets
11. Admission
12. Many of Mrs. Putnam's have died
13. Examination of evidence to determine guilt or innocence
16. John's wife
17. Alone; not as a member of a group
18. Story written to be performed on stage
20. He arrests Elizabeth
21. Play division
23. Material proof
24. Mr. Corey
26. The Creator
27. He thinks of a test for Mary
28. The judge for many witchcraft trials
29. Rebecca
31. Ghosts; beings
35. Opposite of bad

# CROSSWORD ANSWER KEY - *The Crucible*

# MATCHING QUIZ/WORKSHEET 1 - *The Crucible*

___ 1. Pretense              A. John; he tries to make people see the truth

___ 2. Parris                B. He arrests Elizabeth

___ 3. Books                 C. To adore

___ 4. Babies                D. He thinks of a test for Mary

___ 5. Play                  E. Ghosts; beings

___ 6. Putnam                F. Parris wanted a deed and this along with his salary

___ 7. Cheever               G. Betty's father and Abigail's uncle

___ 8. Devil                 H. Many of Mrs. Putnam's have died

___ 9. Firewood              I. Ann or Thomas

___ 10. Act                  J. Decision maker in court

___ 11. Abigail              K. He was an expert spirit remover

___ 12. Judge                L. Mr. Corey

___ 13. Hawthorne            M. Object of the Putnams' dispute with the Nurses

___ 14. Worship              N. The judge for many witchcraft trials

___ 15. Proctor              O. The act of pretending

___ 16. Land                 P. She is the primary cause of the witch hunts

___ 17. Danforth             Q. Play division

___ 18. Spirits              R. Reading material

___ 19. Giles                S. Story written to be performed on stage

___ 20. Hale                 T. Satan

# MATCHING QUIZ/WORKSHEET 2 - *The Crucible*

___ 1. Hawthorne     A. Parris' slave woman from Barbados

___ 2. Witch     B. Black magic; sorcery

___ 3. Act     C. He was an expert spirit remover

___ 4. Parris     D. Woman who practices witchcraft

___ 5. Tituba     E. Betty's father and Abigail's uncle

___ 6. Proctor     F. Meeting place of Tituba and the devil

___ 7. Books     G. Alone; not as a member of a group

___ 8. Witchcraft     H. She wants Abby to tell the truth

___ 9. Mary     I. Rebecca

___ 10. Church     J. He thinks of a test for Mary

___ 11. Danforth     K. John; he tries to make people see the truth

___ 12. Poppet     L. The judge for many witchcraft trials

___ 13. Nurse     M. Gift from Mary to Elizabeth

___ 14. Spirits     N. Move with rhythm

___ 15. Guilt     O. Ghosts; beings

___ 16. Forest     P. Reading material

___ 17. Hale     Q. Bad

___ 18. Dance     R. God's house

___ 19. Evil     S. Play division

___ 20. Individual     T. Conscience's nagging feeling

# KEY: MATCHING QUIZ/WORKSHEETS - *The Crucible*

| **Worksheet 1** | **Worksheet 2** |
|---|---|
| 1. O | 1. J |
| 2. G | 2. D |
| 3. R | 3. S |
| 4. H | 4. E |
| 5. S | 5. A |
| 6. I | 6. K |
| 7. B | 7. P |
| 8. T | 8. B |
| 9. F | 9. H |
| 10. Q | 10. R |
| 11. P | 11. L |
| 12. J | 12. M |
| 13. D | 13. I |
| 14. C | 14. O |
| 15. A | 15. T |
| 16. M | 16. F |
| 17. N | 17. C |
| 18. E | 18. N |
| 19. L | 19. Q |
| 20. K | 20. G |

## JUGGLE LETTER REVIEW GAME CLUE SHEET - *The Crucible*

| SCRAMBLED | WORD | CLUE |
| --- | --- | --- |
| ISNG | SIGN | Something that shows the existence of a fact |
| OSLU | SOUL | If Proctor tells the truth, he will save his |
| TPOEPP | POPPET | Gift from Mary to Elizabeth |
| EHAL | HALE | He was an expert spirit remover |
| KOSBO | BOOKS | Reading material |
| LTZEIABHE | ELIZABETH | John's wife |
| RATLI | TRIAL | Examination of evidence to determine guilt or innocence |
| AESBIB | BABIES | Many of Mrs. Putnam's have died |
| ESECN | SCENE | Division of an act |
| OESNOGSD | GOODNESS | Rebecca is full of it |
| EYBTT | BETTY | Parris' daughter |
| HHCCRU | CHURCH | God's house |
| IELV | EVIL | Bad |
| ERVEECH | CHEEVER | He arrests Elizabeth |
| UGJED | JUDGE | Decision-maker in court |
| HWCIT | WITCH | Woman who practices witchcraft |
| ELIBB | BIBLE | Christian Holy Book |
| CHFTARWTIC | WITCHCRAFT | Black magic; sorcery |
| SETOFR | FOREST | Meeting place of Tituba and the devil |
| EFOWRIDO | FIREWOOD | Parris wanted a deed and this along with his salary |
| FNEIOCSNSO | CONFESSION | Admission |
| ILEVD | DEVIL | Satan |
| LTGUI | GUILT | Conscience's nagging feeling |
| AYLP | PLAY | Story written to be performed on stage |
| NAUPMT | PUTNAM | Ann or Thomas |
| ESENRTPE | PRETENSE | The act of pretending |
| BCECRAE | REBECCA | Mrs. Nurse |
| DIIDUAVNLI | INDIVIDUAL | Alone; not as a member of a group |
| TAC | ACT | Play division |
| ULTRADYE | ADULTERY | Commandment Proctor forgets |
| ALDN | LAND | Object of dispute between Nurses & Putnams |
| UBIATT | TITUBA | Parris' slave woman from Barbados RBE- |
| TIT | BITTER | T. Putnam was this about his situation in life |
| GALBIAI | ABIGAIL | She is the primary cause of the witch hunts |
| SINCFAR | FRANCIS | Mr. Nurse |
| ISELG | GILES | Mr. Corey |
| NIVECEED | EVIDENCE | Material proof |

# VOCABULARY RESOURCE MATERIALS

# VOCABULARY WORD SEARCH - *The Crucible*

```
C G B T A N A R C H Y B T F B N D N E C
L T F L B F E Y B O V G P W A J U L C N
Y A W B S L Y T E E N F J N S K A S N T
D D I A B O L I S M G J E V E I R P E R
M B A I H P S M N A E U U S Q O F D D F
Q Y D B Y E S Y E E R N I R L S A B I X
U U A L P R E N T L R C A L E V W P V R
A C M A O P L O E L X T A C E D A M O M
I A A S C L E N R Y Q P S S I R V V R W
L L N P R E S A P U F T Y J T N R F P X
D U T H I X R Q A Z A X M I P I G P T M
W M V E T E O L G T C P S L R M C L D M
K N D M E D M V I S T A T U T E S A Y X
R Y K Y S R E C R I N E P T L Y B T L Q
A V I D L Y R M A N I F E S T Z Z D X S
```

ADAMANT
ANARCHY
ANONYMITY
AUDIBLE
AVIDLY
BASE
BEGUILE
BLASPHEMY
CALUMNY
CONJURED
DAFT
DIABOLISM
ECSTATIC
EVADE
FRAUD
HYPOCRITES

INEPTLY
INERT
MANIFEST
MENACINGLY
PALLOR
PARTISAN
PERPLEXED
PRETENSE
PROVIDENCE
QUAIL
QUALM
REMORSELESSLY
REPRIEVE
SARCASTICAL
STATUTES

# VOCABULARY WORD SEARCH ANSWER KEY - *The Crucible*

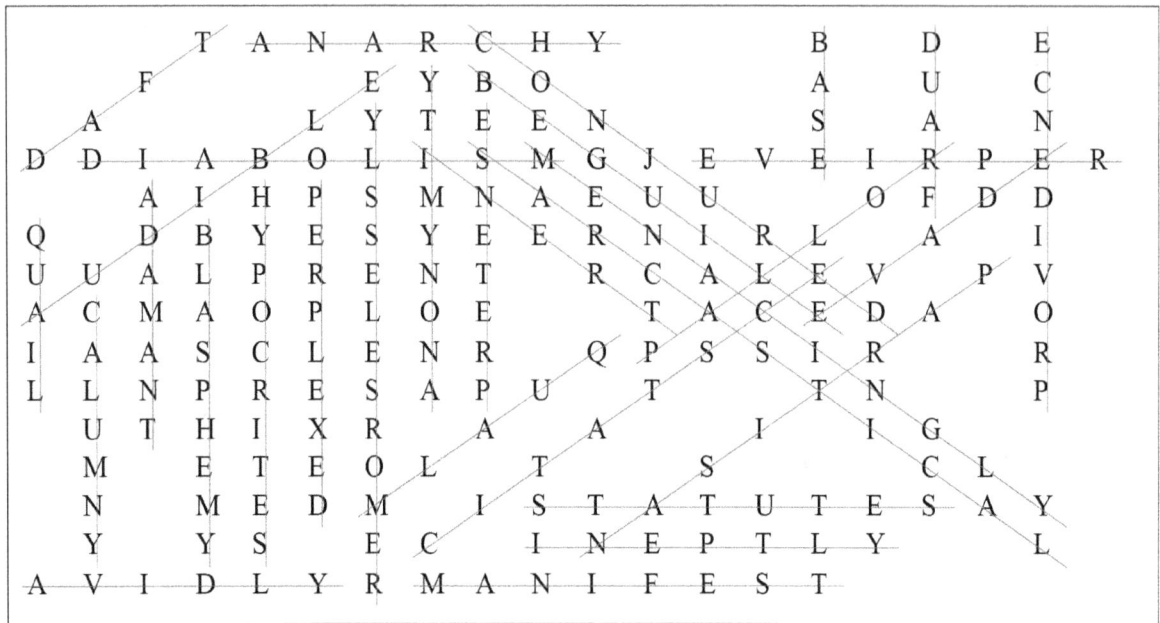

ADAMANT
ANARCHY
ANONYMITY
AUDIBLE
AVIDLY
BASE
BEGUILE
BLASPHEMY
CALUMNY
CONJURED
DAFT
DIABOLISM
ECSTATIC
EVADE
FRAUD
HYPOCRITES

INEPTLY
INERT
MANIFEST
MENACINGLY
PALLOR
PARTISAN
PERPLEXED
PRETENSE
PROVIDENCE
QUAIL
QUALM
REMORSELESSLY
REPRIEVE
SARCASTICAL
STATUTES

## VOCABULARY CROSSWORD - *The Crucible*

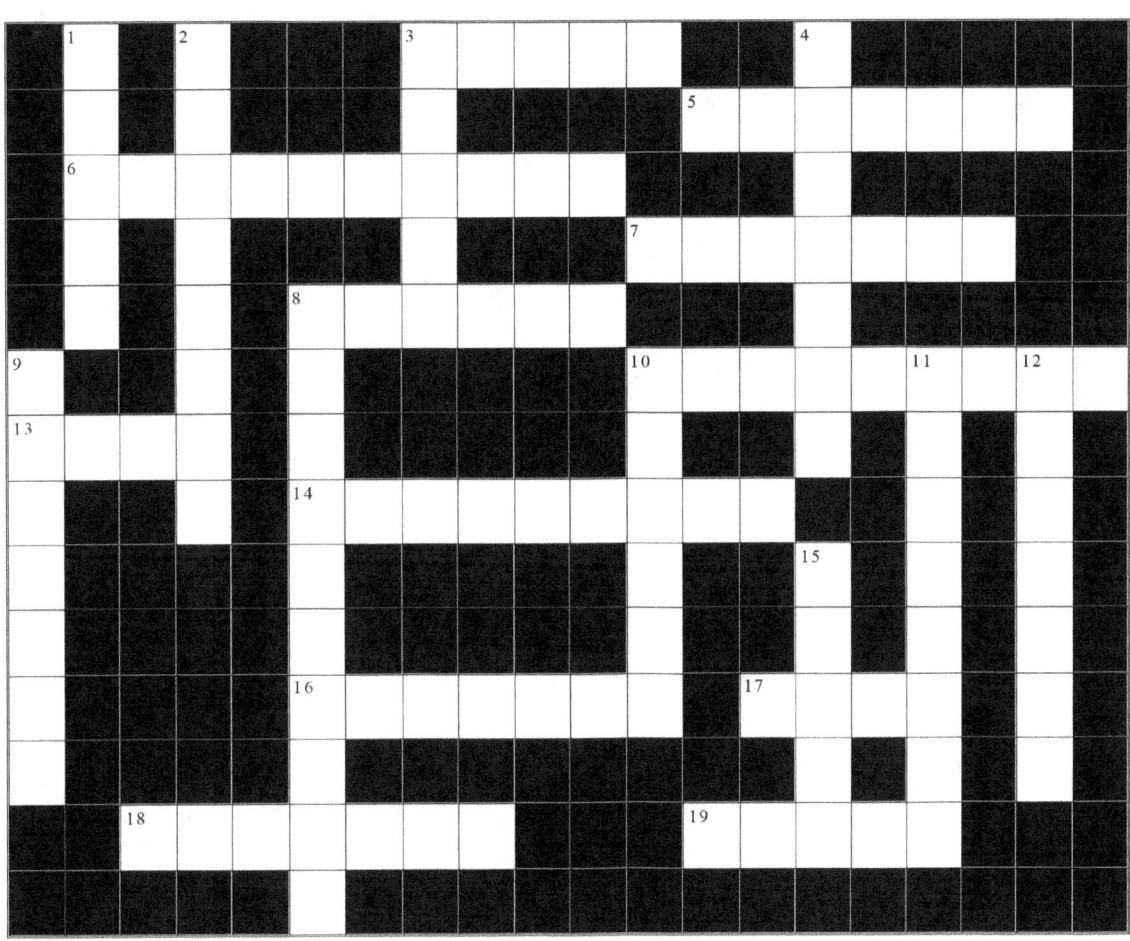

Across
- 3. Sensation of misgiving or uneasiness
- 5. Political disorder and confusion
- 6. Loyalty
- 7. Confused
- 8. Extreme paleness
- 10. Secrecy; having unknown or unacknowledged name
- 13. Crazy; foolish; stupid
- 14. Witchcraft; sorcery
- 16. Awkward
- 17. Having low moral standards; contemptible; inferior
- 18. Delude; cheat; divert
- 19. Unable to move or act

Down
- 1. Deliberate deception for unfair or unlawful gain
- 2. Disaster
- 3. To lose courage; decline; fail; give way
- 4. False statement maliciously or knowingly made to injure someone
- 8. Extraordinary; marvelous
- 9. Firm in purpose or opinion; unyielding
- 10. Enthusiastically
- 11. Something apparent to the sight or understanding
- 12. Having a moral defect; infected
- 15. Escape or avoid by cleverness or deceit

# VOCABULARY CROSSWORD ANSWER KEY - *The Crucible*

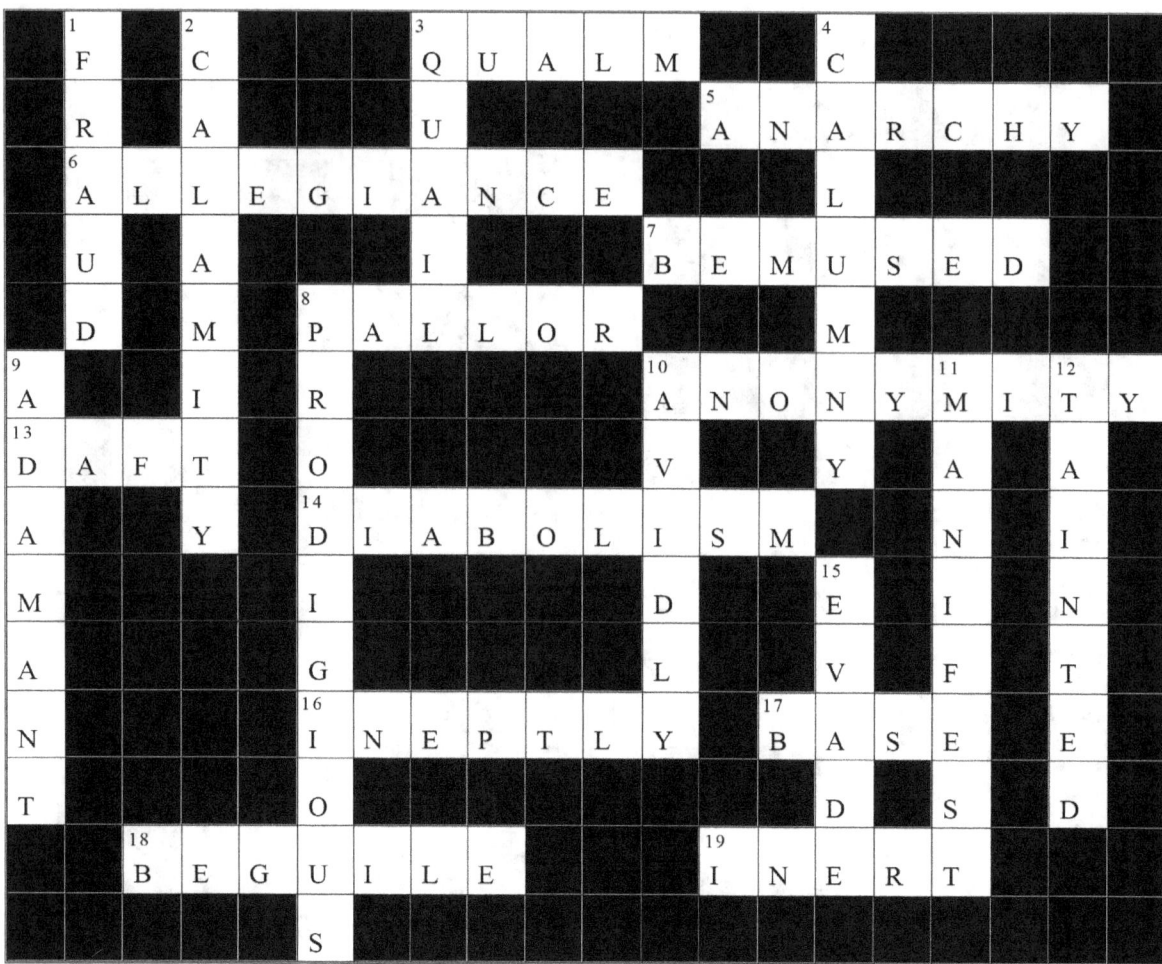

Across
- 3. Sensation of misgiving or uneasiness
- 5. Political disorder and confusion
- 6. Loyalty
- 7. Confused
- 8. Extreme paleness
- 10. Secrecy; having unknown or unacknowledged name
- 13. Crazy; foolish; stupid
- 14. Witchcraft; sorcery
- 16. Awkward
- 17. Having low moral standards; contemptible; inferior
- 18. Delude; cheat; divert
- 19. Unable to move or act

Down
- 1. Deliberate deception for unfair or unlawful gain
- 2. Disaster
- 3. To lose courage; decline; fail; give way
- 4. False statement maliciously or knowingly made to injure someone
- 8. Extraordinary; marvelous
- 9. Firm in purpose or opinion; unyielding
- 10. Enthusiastically
- 11. Something apparent to the sight or understanding
- 12. Having a moral defect; infected
- 15. Escape or avoid by cleverness or deceit

# VOCABULARY WORKSHEET 1 - *The Crucible*

___ 1. Menacingly         A. In a state of exalted delight

___ 2. Penitence          B. Promiscuity

___ 3. Conjured           C. An irreverent or impious act or utterance

___ 4. Blasphemy          D. Extraordinary; marvelous

___ 5. Contemplation      E. Performing of penance

___ 6. Condemnation       F. Work of divine direction

___ 7. Partisan           G. False statement maliciously or knowingly made to injure someone

___ 8. Faction            H. Things that elicit great dislike or abhorrence

___ 9. Ecstatic           I. Escape or avoid by cleverness or deceit

___ 10. Diabolism         J. Witchcraft; sorcery

___ 11. Calumny           K. Small group of people, usually contentious, within a larger group

___ 12. Abominations      L. Militant supporter of a cause, faction or idea

___ 13. Evade             M. Thoughtful observation or meditation

___ 14. Providence        N. Disbelievingly

___ 15. Pretense          O. Severe reproof; strong censure

___ 16. Lechery           P. Threateningly

___ 17. Adamant           Q. The act of pretending

___ 18. Prodigious        R. Summoned by oath or spell

___ 19. Incredulously     S. Having low moral standards; contemptible; inferior

___ 20. Base              T. Firm in purpose or opinion; unyielding

# VOCABULARY WORKSHEET 2 - *The Crucible*

___ 1. Allegiance          A. Laws, decrees or edicts

___ 2. Quail               B. Extreme paleness

___ 3. Licentious          C. Able to be heard

___ 4. Audible             D. Mercilessly; having no pity or compassion

___ 5. Pallor              E. Crazy; foolish; stupid

___ 6. Abominations        F. Confused

___ 7. Sarcastical         G. Loyalty

___ 8. Statutes            H. Quarrelsome

___ 9. Daft                I. Postponement of punishment

___ 10. Contentious        J. The act of pretending

___ 11. Ecstatic           K. Political disorder and confusion

___ 12. Pretense           L. In a state of exalted delight

___ 13. Antagonists        M. To lose courage; decline; fail; give way

___ 14. Prodigious         N. Adversaries; opponents

___ 15. Bemused            O. Extraordinary; marvelous

___ 16. Providence         P. False statement maliciously or knowingly made to injure someone

___ 17. Calumny            Q. Things that elicit great dislike or abhorrence

___ 18. Anarchy            R. Having no regard for accepted rules or standards

___ 19. Remorselessly      S. Expressing mocking or contemptuous remarks

___ 20. Reprieve           T. Work of divine direction

# KEY: VOCABULARY WORKSHEETS - *The Crucible*

| **Worksheet 1** | **Worksheet 2** |
|---|---|
| 1. P | 1. G |
| 2. E | 2. M |
| 3. R | 3. R |
| 4. C | 4. C |
| 5. M | 5. B |
| 6. O | 6. Q |
| 7. L | 7. S |
| 8. K | 8. A |
| 9. A | 9. E |
| 10. J | 10. H |
| 11. G | 11. L |
| 12. H | 12. J |
| 13. I | 13. N |
| 14. F | 14. O |
| 15. Q | 15. F |
| 16. B | 16. T |
| 17. T | 17. P |
| 18. D | 18. K |
| 19. N | 19. D |
| 20. S | 20. I |

## VOCABULARY JUGGLE LETTER REVIEW GAME CLUES - *The Crucible*

| SCRAMBLED | WORD | CLUE |
| --- | --- | --- |
| IELGEUB | BEGUILE | Delude; cheat; divert |
| ILVYAD | AVIDLY | Enthusiastically |
| OIENUTNCSOT | CONTENTIOUS | Quarrelsome |
| ELRSYEOERSLSM | REMORSELESSLY | Mercilessly; having no pity or compassion |
| UMLAQ | QUALM | Sensation of misgiving or uneasiness |
| BIALEDU | AUDIBLE | Able to be heard |
| ERECYLH | LECHERY | Promiscuity |
| NIAFTCO | FACTION | Small group of people, usually contentious, within a larger group |
| ECRUODJN | CONJURED | Summoned by oath or spell |
| YANCARH | ANARCHY | Political disorder or confusion |
| DETTANI | TAINTED | Having a moral defect; infected |
| NDNNTAEICOMO | CONDEMNATION | Severe reproof; strong censure |
| ARPANTSI | PARTISAN | Militant supporter of a cause, faction or idea |
| ERREEVPI | REPRIEVE | Postponement of punishment |
| IMTYLACA | CALAMITY | Disaster |
| GNEYLMANCI | MENACINGLY | Threateningly |
| YNMLCUA | CALUMNY | False statement knowingly made to injure someone |
| REPEDPLEX | PERPLEXED | Bewildered; puzzled; confused |
| LIQAU | QUAIL | To lose courage; decline; fail |
| PYMLHSBAE | BLASPHEMY | An irreverent or impious act or utterance |
| TNAAEIRSC | ASCERTAIN | Find out |
| LNCONOMITAETP | CONTEMPLATION | Thoughtful observation or meditation |
| VEENDOCRIP | PROVIDENCE | Work of divine direction |
| TPNYLEI | INEPTLY | Awkwardly |
| ASXRIETDFN | TRANSFIXED | Rendered motionless with terror, amazement or awe |
| SNTOTIGSANA | ANTAGONISTS | Adversaries; opponents |
| EMTOONUPSTCU | CONTEMPTUOUS | Scornful; disdainful |
| RDUAF | FRAUD | Deliberate deception for unfair or unlawful gain |
| SEHRIYCOPT | HYPOCRITES | People who say they believe one way but in actions show otherwise |
| ASEB | BASE | Having low moral standards; contemptible; inferior |
| EDBSEUM | BEMUSED | Confused |

*Crucible* Juggle Letter Vocabulary Review Game Clues Continued

| | | |
|---|---|---|
| ETCNEEPIN | PENITENCE | Performing of penance |
| NYTOEREFFR | EFFRONTERY | Audacity; insulting boldness |
| ANTADMA | ADAMANT | Firm in purpose or opinion; unyielding |
| ININDNTGA | INDIGNANT | Filled with anger aroused by something unjust or unworthy |
| IULTCSOIEN | LICENTIOUS | Having no regard for accepted rules or standards |
| TESUSATT | STATUTES | Laws, decrees, or edicts |
| SNFATMIE | MANIFEST | Something apparent to the sight or understanding |
| YMTYAINON | ANONYMITY | Secrecy; having unknown or unacknowledged name |
| IOPURODISG | PRODIGIOUS | Extraordinary; marvelous |
| TIMNAOBIOSAN | ABOMINATIONS | Things that elicit great dislike or abhorrence |
| TIOITAPOPNRI | PROPITIATION | Appeasement |
| OLLARP | PALLOR | Extreme paleness |

www.ingramcontent.com/pod-product-compliance
Lightning Source LLC
Chambersburg PA
CBHW051415070526
44584CB00023B/3436